ENDORSEMENTS

"Desi's book aims to breathe life into lifeless workplaces through humor, heart, and honest observations. She's on a mission to inject positivity into every leader—and the people they lead!"

—Mark Cole, CEO, John Maxwell Enterprises

"It turns out the zombies aren't here to eat our brains. They're here to tell us how busy they are, whine that there's no cake in the break room, and count the hours until Friday. Desi Payne's witty comparison of the zombie apocalypse and the workplace downer is a fun read with actionable strategies to survive the work day!"

—Paul Osincup,
TedX Speaker & Positive Workplace Strategist

"In today's complex, competitive working environment, it takes the entire team to make things go. Desi Payne has taken some complex issues on motivating the team and creating a positive, productive working environment and distilled them down to easily actionable strategies that leaders can use immediately. If you're a leader wanting to make a difference, I highly recommend Desi's book *Do You Work with the Living Dead?* You'll walk away from reading it with a new lease on work life."

—Lieutenant Commander Chip Lutz,
United States Navy (Retired), MSEd, CSP, CHP

"With stress and information overload on the rise, it's easy to feel like we're constantly running on empty. Desi Payne takes a serious problem and engages readers with humor to emphasize the magnitude of where we're heading if we don't take serious action soon. Read this book, and recharge your life."

—Dr. Heidi Hanna, PhD, NY Times best-selling author
and founder of the Stress Mastery Academy

DO YOU
WORK
WITH THE
LIVING
DE🧟D?

Desi Payne

DO YOU WORK WITH THE LIVING DEAD?

SURVIVING AMONG NEGATIVE AND LIFELESS PEOPLE IN THE WORKPLACE

DESI PAYNE

AUTHOR ACADEMY elite

Published by Author Academy Elite
P. O. Box 43, Powell, OH 43065
www.AuthorAcademyElite.com

Permission granted by Penguin Random House for excerpt from *Heal Your Heart* by Michael Miller, M.D.

Artwork: Angel Contreras
Cover design: Rakesh Ghosh
Interior design: JetLaunch.net

Paperback: 978-1-64085-764-3
Hardback: 978-1-64085-765-0
eBook: 978-1-64085-766-7

Library of Congress Control Number: 2019909275

Available in hardcover, softcover, eBook, and audiobook.

ACKNOWLEDGEMENTS

There are so many people in my life who have infected me with their enthusiastic attitude that I couldn't even begin to list them. Plus, if I left someone out, I wouldn't want him or her to turn into a zombie. But I do want to acknowledge my husband, Craig, who has graciously and with a wonderful attitude spent countless hours editing my book and giving me his expert advice.

CONTENTS

PART 3: WHAT IF YOU GET INFECTED BY THE LIVING DEAD?

PART 4: WILL YOU CHOOSE TO BE DEAD OR ALIVE?

FOREWORD

Do You Work with the Living Dead? is a guide to thriving when dealing with negative and lifeless people in the workplace. Desi Payne offers a thoughtful and insightful look into the realities of working in a high-stress company with high-stress people. You will spend 90,000 hours or 1/3 of your life working. According to the International Labor Organization (ILO), more than 2.3 million workers die every year around the world as a result of occupational accidents or work-related diseases. To put this number in perspective, across the world 167,000 people died in armed conflicts in 2015, according to the latest edition of the IISS Armed Conflict Survey. In addition to this astounding number, each year 313 million accidents occur on the job, resulting in extended absences from work.

The ILO estimates that the annual cost to the global economy from accidents and work-related diseases alone is a staggering $3 trillion. Moreover, a recent report suggests the world's 3.2 billion workers are increasingly unwell, with the vast majority facing significant economic insecurity: 77% work in part-time, temporary, "vulnerable," or unpaid jobs. What's more, the labor force is growing older and less healthy: 52% is overweight or obese and 38% suffers from excessive pressure on the job.

In short, Desi Payne's book is timely and is a must read for anyone who has a job or is an employer! As part of her Zombie survival guide, she has a list of Zombie traits that will make you acutely aware of the zombies you work with. You will start to identify the Zombie traits that you yourself have so you do not end up being one of the "living dead." On top of that, she gives you the Zombie actions to watch out for... because anyone who has watched one of the numerous Zombie television shows will want to make sure to spot the traits and actions so you can keep yourself safe and growing without turning into a Zombie yourself!

Desi Payne does more than identify the problem or the symptoms; she has strategies to deal with Zombies, CPR strategies, and ways to reboot the Zombie Brain! While the main theme of the book helps you learn many ways that humor helps you deal with Zombies, and how to keep yourself from becoming a Zombie....you will find your heart deeply touched as she shares her experiences in dealing with death and dying. Her stories not only teach, they help you keep your heart alive in a world that at times seems to be turning you into another Zombie.

I hope CEO's and owners of companies buy this book by the case to give to each employee. Stress-related illness, workman' s comp costs, and absenteeism will go down as laughter, gratitude, and humor go up. If you are not an owner or CEO, you will find yourself recommending this book to your boss and encouraging him or her to bring Desi in as speaker or consultant. After all, don't you want how you spend 1/3 of your life on earth to bring meaning to the other 2/3 of your life? Happier Workplaces = Happier Homes= a changed society. Read this book and share it with others. Keep those around you from turning into a bunch of Zombies!

Dr. Earl R. Henslin, Psy.D., B.C.E.T.S.
Board Certified Expert in Traumatic Stress
Diplomate in the American Academy of Experts in
Traumatic Stress
Author, *This Is Your Brain on Joy* & *This Is Your Brain on Love*

PART 1

WHO ARE THE LIVING DEAD?

CHAPTER 1

NEGATIVE TRAITS OF THE LIVING DEAD

Have they overtaken the world?

"I see dead people."

—Cole Sear, *The Sixth Sense*

One evening as I walked through our family room, I was shocked when I witnessed an axe fly through the air and hit someone in the head. Brain matter and blood spurted out everywhere. My stomach did a belly-flop as I turned to my husband and daughter, who also witnessed the axe incident. I asked them in a rather high-pitched voice, "What on earth are you watching?" They were intently watching the TV screen and didn't blink an eye as one of them mumbled, "*The Walking Dead.*" Since I usually can't stomach anything violent, scary, or bloody, I walked out of the room shaking my head.

Little did I know at the time, it was a popular, Emmy-winning, horror drama series. Many of you may be big fans of the show. If you don't know what it's about, it features a guy by the name of Rick Grimes who wakes up in the hospital from a coma to find the world infected with a virus resulting in zombies. On the show they are called "walkers." I never did get into the show, again due to my low tolerance of blood and guts flying through the air as a result of an arrow, knife, axe, or some other type of sharp blade entering into the skulls of the zombies. From what I understand from the die-hard fans (okay, no pun intended, but I had to say that), they are very absorbed in the story. From season to season I hear discussions about what people had watched. Some people are disappointed when their friends or family members spoil who had recently died on the show. (I know enough to know that no one wants Darryl to die.)

One day when I again walked through the family room and saw those zombies dragging themselves through the streets, it reminded me of Cole Sear in the movie *The Sixth Sense*, in particular the moment Cole reveals his secret: "I see dead people."

So now I must reveal *my* secret:

I see the living dead.

The living dead are people who are alive, yet remind me of zombies because they act exactly like them. They are people I used to work with, people I see when I'm working in different venues, people I see in various occupations in different types of establishments (which I won't single out).

Certainly you know who I'm talking about: Those people who drag themselves slowly into work, moaning and groaning about everything from the weather to their workload. They are the people who bite and devour one another with their words and infect people with their negativity. The bottom line is this: The living dead are people who live life without any enthusiasm, people whose lives center around their negative attitudes. I'll bet your wheels are turning; you're thinking of particular individuals right now. They might even be some of your relatives. Whatever you do, don't say their names out loud!

Since I've never been a zombie fan or been concerned about a zombie apocalypse, I've needed to do my research on zombies to discover their most common characteristics. In general, zombies move slowly, growl, moan, or groan, drag themselves in and out of places, have poor hygiene, dress sloppily, are hungry all the time, always think of their next meal, bite, devour, don't talk, have no personality, slouch, and display poor people skills. Some are isolated, while some travel in herds. They have blank stares, but can be aggressive, selfish, and mean. Again, did you notice that some of these are characteristics of people who have negative attitudes in the workplace and even in their personal lives? Perhaps even people you know?

All of us have worked with people who grate at us and get on our nerves. They get nicknames like Nurse Ratched, Cyborg T-1000, Agent Smith, Cruella de Vil, Voldemort, Palpatine, or perhaps even Darth Vader. Without thinking, you mumble those names under your breath, catching yourself before saying them out loud at the wrong moment (usually).

We've all encountered people even outside our workplace who rub us the wrong way. They are the people who wait on us, whether it's at a store, a restaurant, a ticket counter, a checkout lane, a service station, or any type of customer service situation. These people have glazed eyes and no smile. After they drag themselves over to you and take your order, you want to ask them, "What is your problem?" Again, these people are like the living dead. They act cold and remote; they are tired most of the time; they have no enthusiasm for life. When you think about it, dead people don't go anywhere. When you're one of the living dead, shuffling through life, acting dead, you won't go anywhere in life either. In other words, your success rate is pretty low.

The living dead remind me of "Joy-Suckers." You can feel the joy being sucked out of a room when you hear the workplace zombies say things like:

It will never work.

Whatever.

We've tried that before.

We've always done it this way.

Did you hear about so and so?

Who made that decision?

Don't call me, I'll call you.

I can't believe they expect us to do that.

It's not my job.

I'm too old.

I'm not smart enough.

I can't do it.

I don't know how to do it.

Did you see what she's wearing?

I remember a workplace zombie at my husband's employment. Whenever Craig (my husband) would go to work and see him waiting in his office or coming down the hallway, his heart would sink; he really didn't want to talk with him. This workplace zombie would have the latest gossip about employees; he was very negative about administration, had a bad attitude toward the community, knew how much every person on the faculty made (it was a public school with public records), and compared those salaries to his. Of course, he had something negative to say about all of these things, and, bottom line, he wasted Craig's time. Craig always did his best to deflect the conversation, change it, or try to throw something positive in the mix. Unfortunately, this was draining—it not only zapped his energy, but was a huge waste of his time.

Co-workers who also dreaded this workplace zombie created a code amongst each other. If they knew the guy was in Employee X's office, other employees would call X and X would say on the telephone, "Oh, hi. Is it that time already? I'll be right there." It's very sad when employees have to resort to trickery to defend themselves from another employee.

The guy, whom I'll call Agent Z, no longer works at the college—but something happened which was both funny and sad. Agent Z got a different position at a different college in a neighboring state. In a few years, representatives from that college came on a tour through my husband's college. They knew Agent Z had formerly been employed at Craig's college, and, while walking through the hallways, one of them whispered to a faculty member who was a friend of my husband: "Do you want him back?"

Like I said, funny—but sad.

You probably could tell stories like me of your encounters with the living dead. Recently, my videographer friend, Isaac, who is probably in the top ten most enthusiastic people I know, was involved in a huge downtown renovation celebration. He poured his heart into art murals and photography that would beautify our downtown. After a very hard rain, unfortunately one of the murals started falling apart and was hanging in shreds off the side of one of the buildings. After countless hours of trying to polish the city with a great appearance, Isaac was sad that all that hard work came to ruin. But he was even sadder when someone emerged from the dead and took a picture of the mural hanging in shreds, posted it on Facebook and wrote, "Well isn't that fabulous... didn't take long for the side of one of the newly refurbished buildings to get ruined! Nice job Main Street! #fail." It's very disheartening when people are negative and especially when they attack you. Isaac chose not to respond, and of course cleaned up the shredded mural as soon as he could.

I too have experienced attacks from the living dead. It's hard to comprehend why people act the way they do. I remember when I had applied for a grant with Fed Ex to do some educational programs in schools. To win, I needed thousands of votes. I posted on Facebook that I needed votes to win this grant contest. I was overwhelmed with the community support. However, one person in the community, whom I'll call a "Biting Zombie" (I'll talk about them more later in the book), criticized me for asking for the votes. He didn't think I should receive money if I went into a school to do a program. Of course, I tried to explain to him that I would be teaching students about respect and bully-prevention. Mistake! The person continued to bite at me (he didn't think speakers for school children should take money for speaking). Instead of biting back and asking how *he* made a living, I decided to delete him from the post and remember that there are always zombies lurking in your neighborhood, ready to attack.

I've noticed an interesting reaction that occurs whenever I even bring up the title of this book. People perk up and are ready to share their stories of the living dead. For example, a director of a child care center for over twenty years shared her thoughts on these types of people in the workplace. She felt people are more negative today and act "dead" more than ever before. She said years ago, employees would arrive for work as scheduled because that's what you're supposed to do. Nowadays, they don't show up, no phone call, no text, absolutely nothing to indicate why they wouldn't show up to work. When asked about talking with employees with negative attitudes, she responded that many times they would just look at her with that zombie-like "glazed" look and act like they really don't care. She told me about employees who are "ghosting"—the first time I had heard that term. I learned that ghosting takes place when a person abruptly goes silent or disappears without explanation. According to a recent LinkedIn article by Chip Cutter, "People are 'ghosting' at work and it's driving companies crazy." For example, candidates who have agreed to job interviews fail to show up without any notice or further communication and, in some cases, accept jobs but don't show up for their first day of work. My husband says the same thing is happening now with students who make appointments with faculty but do not meet with them. That doesn't make any sense to me. What happened to a society of respect and responsibility? It seems "ghosts" and "zombies" go hand in hand.

The director also said that many people have grown up with parents who have negative attitudes and do not have a strong work ethic, so it's been passed down to the next generation. Having a poor work ethic certainly shows up in a person's attitude. Since I've always had a strong work ethic, I know that I inherited that from my mother, who taught me the importance of working hard, but she got it from her mother, who knew that no work equals no food on the table.

My mother has owned restaurants for over thirty years and she's seen a shift in the way employees perform. Many don't know how to count back change, they don't see things that need to be done until they're told to do them, and their attitudes are negative toward working and life in general.

Yesterday while shopping at a mall, I noticed several people in their pajama bottoms shopping. It wasn't the first time I had seen people neglect to change their clothes after they got up to present themselves in public places. Really? Do people have such an attitude of laziness that they can't change into their day clothes? Or do they have too much on their minds? (Somehow, I doubt that one.) Or are they simply showing the rest of us that they have so little respect for us, they can't even be bothered with dressing?

When I was in a restaurant not too long ago, a very young hostess was telling me how she really wanted to get another job, one with better pay. I encouraged her to apply for the job she was interested in, but she responded quickly in her nasal, whiney voice, "But I'd have to fill out so much paperwork again." I wanted to respond with, "Okay, you lazy zombie, stay where you're at for the rest of your life."

Lazy and irresponsible attitudes are quite common, of course. Probably we all have our own stories. However, an attitude which is even more common is simple negativity.

I will discuss this more later in the book, but when people have a negative attitude there usually is a reason for it. A few years ago, I was performing as a magician in a school. It was an evening program, and my assistant and I had driven many hours to get there. The student counselor had hired me to do my bully-prevention program. While we were setting up, the school's principal was there, but seemed very disengaged and even unfriendly. One of my props had broken, so while fixing it, I asked her if we could start five minutes late. To this she replied very sharply, "Whatever!" I was startled by the response.

As she was about to introduce me to the students, she came behind the stage and abruptly said, "I really don't want to be here tonight because I'm missing my daughter's volleyball game." I apologized, and after she went out front to introduce me with no enthusiasm or really any emotion at all, I thought, "Oh boy, here we go." I didn't look at her during the show and did all I could to stay focused on performing a great show for everyone. Many times, you must look beneath the surface to see why people act the way they do. Negativity can be caused by underlying anger or other unresolved issues.

It doesn't matter what occupation people have, what income level, what status in society, or what age, you will find folks with negative and bad attitudes in all workplaces.

Why do people get bad attitudes? The first one you've heard many times is this silly excuse: "I woke up on the wrong side of the bed." I always wondered why one side would make you negative and the other side happy. At any rate, there are countless reasons to get in a bad mood. Here are a few: Not feeling well, doing something you don't want to do, watching others get promoted, being treated unfairly, having no money in the bank account, clashing with people, getting stuck in traffic, enduring boring meetings, having a bad hair day, caring for a sick child, receiving lousy service, not getting your way, having to visit someone you don't want to visit, not feeling liked, waiting in a long line, discovering a dent in your car, having something stolen from you, getting a speeding ticket (that usually doubles the bad mood), disliking the weather, your sports team losing, being overweight, feeling unattractive, not being served the right food in a restaurant, feeling unaccepted, undergoing stress, not fitting in, or sometimes hanging around other people in a bad mood. (Moods and attitudes are contagious!)

When I'm training employees in the workplace about the living dead with negative attitudes, I ask them to get into groups to write down the traits of a negative person in the work-

Many times, you must look beneath the surface to see why people act the way they do.

place. It doesn't take long for people to quickly compile a list. They come alive and get a burst of energy as they talk about what they see in OTHER people. Apparently, the zombies in the workplace lurk everywhere. Let's look at the traits of people with dead or negative attitudes. (You don't have to read all of them; my point is simply to show you how employees come up with so many traits of their co-workers.)

TRAITS (Some of these contradict each other; the traits are not always exhibited at the same time)—Workplace Zombies are:

Abusive
Afraid to get out of their
   comfort zones
Aggressive
Always expecting the worst
Alone
Always blaming others
Always ready to take a break
   or lunch

Always stressed and
   exhausted
Always worried
Angry
Anxious
Apathetic
Argumentative
Arrogant
Attention-seeking
"Bad apples"

Bad at making choices
Bad-mouthing others
"Blah-Blah-Blah-Blah"
"Blame game"
Bitter, and yet also:
Bland
Bored
Boring
Bossy
Brash
Bullies
Buried in the phone
Bad at taking constructive
  feedback
Catty
Cheaters
Checked-out
Closed-minded
Cloudy-minded
Cold-hearted
Comatose
Combative
Complacent
Complainers
Condescending
Confrontational
Conniving
Consumed with
  social media
Contradictory
Controlling
Convinced of the worst
Crabby
Cranky
Critical

Cry-babies
Cyber-junkies
Cynical
Damaging
Dark clouds
Dead-beats
Debbie Downers (no
  offense to my Debbie
  friends)
Deceitful
Defensive
Deflating
Degrading
Demanding
Demeaning
Depressing
Detrimental
Difficult
Disagreeable
Disconnected
Discouraging
Disengaged
Disgruntled
Dishonest
Disloyal
Disrespectful
Disruptive
Distant
Distracting
Divisive
"Doom and Gloom"
Doubters
Drags others down
Draining
Drama Queens (or Kings)

Dream Killers
Dreary
Drunk
Dull
Dysfunctional
Easily irritated
Emotional
Energy vampires
Excluding of others
Excusing self for all
  problems
Explosive
Eye-rollers
Fabricating
Facebook fanatics
Fault-finding
Finger-pointers
Freeloaders
Frenzied
Friendless
Frowning
"Frumpy"
Glass half-empty kind of
  people
Going through the motions
Gossips
Green with envy
"Grinch"
Grouchy
Growlers
Grumblers
Grumpy
Hard to motivate
Hard to work with
Harsh

Hungry all the time
Hurtful
Hypochondriac
Impatient
In your face
Inconsiderate
Indecisive
Indifferent
Insecure
Insensitive to other's
  feelings
Insulting
Interrupting
Isolated
Jaded
Jealous
Judgmental
Know-It-Alls
Lacking consideration of
  others
Lacks enthusiasm
Late
Lazy
Lethargic
Lifeless
"Life sucks"
Loners
Looks out only for self
Loud
Mad at the world
Makers of excuses
Manipulative
Martyrs
Mean
Mindless

Motionless
Moody
Mumblers
Narcissistic
Nasty
Nay-sayer
Negative in attitude and
comments
"Negative Nancies" (again,
no offense to my Nancy
friends)
Never satisfied
No eye contact
Non-compliant
Non-participating
Not a team player
Not professional
Not reliable
No ownership of projects
or work
No personal interaction
with others
No sense of humor
Not organized
Not serious about work
Not solution-based
Not willing to help
Non-listeners
Non-smilers
Non-volunteering
Never wrong
Nitpickers
Non-productive
Not fun people to be around
Not hard workers

Not team players
Not committed, creative, or
changeable
Not open to ideas
Not prepared
Not responsible
Not well groomed
Not willing to participate
Oblivious to how they come
across
Obstinate
Offensive
Opinionated
Out of ideas
Overly dramatic
Overly outspoken
Overly sensitive
Passive-aggressive
Pessimistic
Playing the victim
Poisoning the environment
Poor at choosing
their words
Poor in attendance
Poor communicators
"Pot-stirrers"
Pouting
Predators
Prickly
Problem employees
Proud
"Real Downers"
Resentful
Resistant to change
Rude

Sad
Sarcastic
"Scrooge"
Secluded
Self-absorbed, self-centered, selfish
Sharp-tongued
Short-tempered
Slackers
Slave drivers of others
Sloppy and slouched
Slow-moving
Sluggish
Snarky
Sneaky
Sound effects/sighing
Sour
Speaking bad about others
Spiteful
Stagnant
Starts arguments
Stone-faced
"Stirs the pot" to provoke trouble
Stressed out with life
Sulky
Swearers
Tactical (crafty in dealing with others)
Talking about others
Talking down to others
Talky when they want to be, usually for no good reason
Tattle-tales
Terrible in their attitudes

Think they can do better than others
Think they know it all
Thin-skinned
Tired
Too "busy" actually to help
Touchy
Toxic
Trouble-makers
Twisters of information
Ugly in actions
Unambitious
Unapproachable
Uncaring
Uncollaborative
Undermining
Under-performing
Unfriendly
Ungrateful
Unhappy
Uninterested
Unkempt
Unkind
Unmotivated
Unproductive
Unprofessional
Unreachable
Unreliable
Unsatisfied
Unstable
Unsupportive
Untrustworthy
Unwilling to help or participate

Unwilling to work with others
Upset most of the time
Vengeful
"Victims" in their own minds
Wanting others to fail
Whiners
Withdrawing
"Zoned out"
Zombies!

So much for the TRAITS of zombies. Now let's list some of the zombies' ACTIONS. (This is only a partial list; the actions of zombies are everywhere to be found.) Zombies like to:

Answer "No" reflexively
Avoid eye contact
Bite and devour other employees
Bite heads off
Blow things out of proportion
Bring personal problems to work
Carry chips on their shoulders
Cause exhaustion and frustration in others
"Check out" mentally
Complicate situations unnecessarily
Dash others' hopes
Do the "Eeyore" moaning
Drag others down
Dress sloppily
Do the bare minimum
Enjoy conflict
Enjoy secrecy
Fail—it shows they were right in the first place
Find the negative in everything
Fix on a particular way of thinking and do not entertain change
Give blank stares
Give poor customer service
Hate being at work
Hate customers
Ignore customers
Lack awareness of environment
Lack drive or motivation
Leave early to make up for arriving late
Make a problem out of non-problems
Make excuses
Make life miserable for others
Never apologize

Never get excited about
anything new
Never laugh unless sneering
at someone else
Never work as a team
member
Not carry his or her
own load
Not have fun
Often ask, "Why me?"
Pass the buck
See the glass as half empty,
as well as cracked
See the world as revolving
around them
Seldom say anything kind
or encouraging
Show zero motivation
Spin a conversation to the
negative
Suck the life out of others
Tell others what to do
Think they are always right
Throw temper tantrums
Treat others with no respect
Vent a lot
Zombify others!
(Remember, being a zom-
bie spreads by biting.)

Wow, that's quite a list! I hope you don't work with anyone who has all of those traits and does all of those actions.
If you do, this book will definitely help you deal with that
person. So, don't despair; we'll get to practical advice soon
(unless you're desperate; in that case, go to Chapter 3 now!)

In the meantime, let's look at people who display the 22
different types of zombie attitudes in the workplace.

CHAPTER 2

ZOMBIES IN THE WORKPLACE

Do you know any of these?

"This is the part in the movie where that guy says,
'Zombies? What zombies?'
Just before they eat his brains. I don't want to be that guy."

—Holly Black, *The Good Neighbors #1: Kin*

The previous chapter introduced us to zombies in the workplace, but now it is time for some specifics. Here is a listing of the 22 different categories of zombie attitudes we can encounter on the job and in life everywhere:

The Moping Zombie:

The definition of mope is to "wander around listlessly and aimlessly because of unhappiness." The moping zombies are people who drag themselves slowly into work; their primary goal for the day is to make it to their day off or (better) payday. Chances are high they surf the internet or visit regularly on some type of social media when they should be working. They're probably looking for another job. They call off from work frequently. When they do show up, they do the minimal amount of work that they have to do. They don't care about people, their job, co-workers, customers, patients, or students. If they work with customers, they provide poor customer service. In fact, the Moping Zombie probably scares customers away. They also don't like to collaborate with other colleagues. A Moping Zombie might not exhibit all of these traits, but does have at least some of them.

People tend to mope for different reasons. They either 1) don't like their jobs, 2) are discouraged or depressed on the job, or 3) do not have their "dream job" yet.

Workplace zombies are disengaged with their workplace. In fact, according to Catherine Clifford, senior writer on entrepreneurship with CNBC, "Disgruntled, disengaged, unsatisfied workers are less productive, less creative, and more likely to leave. Unhappy workers cost the U.S. between $450 billion to 550 billion in lost productivity each year."

After I got out of college, I got a job at a hospital where I felt like a Moping Zombie. I was in charge of payroll, staffing every nurse in the hospital 24/7, and reported to five different people who all wanted their assignments first, yesterday, and now. It was demanding and stressful. I didn't like Sunday nights as I knew what was coming the next morning. Many days I was discouraged as I continually asked myself, friends, family, and even God, "Is THIS what I'm supposed to do with my life?" I needed the job as I was the breadwinner at the time while my husband was in college. Since I needed to stick it out for ten years, I had to adjust my attitude (my husband attended graduate school after college—for a very long time). I'm so glad I changed the attitude and never quit as another door of opportunity finally opened up.

I honestly believe what you're doing today is always preparing you for what you're going to do tomorrow or in your future. At the end of that ten-year period I was promoted to customer service training and became a patient advocate. I absolutely loved the job; the chance to talk with every patient on a daily basis to find out if they were satisfied with their patient care was very fulfilling. Every day was an adventure for me to problem-solve and work with staff to exceed the patient's expectation of care. In that fourteen-year incubation period at the hospital, I learned how to be my own boss, discipline myself to get work done, and handle complaints from angry people. I learned how to read people, speak to groups of people, write material, design marketing materials, be creative, and work under stressful circumstances. All those things prepared me for being my own boss and working with people, which is what I do today. Later, that job led me to a connection with someone who literally changed my life and career.

Again, I am so thankful I never left. I highly encourage you to evaluate and take time to reflect about your own job. Do some soul searching and find out if you should stay and change your attitude or if you should leave your job. As John C. Maxwell says in his book *Leadership Gold*, "You will never fulfill your destiny doing something you despise. Passion will fuel you and give you energy when others around you grow tired."

If you are a leader and you question why people mope, are unhappy with their jobs, or why you have a high turnover, then you need to seriously reflect not only upon their attitudes, but also upon your own leadership skills. I called my mentor and friend, Mark Cole, President of the John Maxwell Company, and asked him about turnover in the workplace. He said, "People generally don't quit jobs; people quit people. Turnover is a result of people not feeling like they matter. I firmly believe people will challenge themselves to do almost anything if they like who they're doing it with."

If you're in a job you don't like, then the options are simple: Quit moping or look for another job. Maybe it is time to make a lifestyle change. Until you find another job, work on getting a better attitude, do your very best at whatever it is you're doing, learn something new, and make the decision that you are going to add value to the people around you. Give it your best; you might be preparing for another job! You never know what doors of opportunity could open internally or externally.

The Biting Zombie:

Biting Zombies are people who have razor-sharp tongues and are critical, sarcastic, fault-finding, cynical, and rude. They constantly bash people in authority and talk about people behind their backs—they are truly "back-biters." Their tongues are very harsh.

Recently I was teaching a special leadership class for students at a high school. The students were excellent, receptive, and engaged. I ended my session by showing them a very inspirational video clip, which the students liked very much. During the video, the teacher started going up and down the aisles frantically throwing a paper on each students' desk. I thought this was a little distracting and rude, but didn't say anything. When the video was over, I told the students I was done and thanked them for their time. The bell rang and the students got up to go to their next class. All of a sudden, the same teacher harshly yelled, "Sit back down! I didn't say you could go!" The students quickly sat back down, and you could hear a pin drop. Wait a minute; you really couldn't hear a pin drop, because the teacher started speaking in her harsh voice to explain what was on the flyer and how the students needed to tell their parents the information.

As my belly did a flip-flop while still standing in the front of the room, my first thought was, "These kids are going to stuff the paper into their backpacks and probably not going to remember to tell their parents about it until they empty their backpacks in a few days" (I know this from experience raising my own kids). Then I thought further: "The Biting Zombie has entered the room." She was so focused on what she needed to get accomplished, she didn't even think to acknowledge or thank me for coming. I felt very bad for these students as this teacher probably daily entered into… "The Zombie Zone." (Please visualize me saying that in Rod Serling's voice.) Interestingly enough, a year later she was fired from her position.

People with sharp tongues are often oblivious to how they come across to other people. On occasion, my husband gives me "the look" if I become the Biting Zombie while in conversation. It's important to pay attention and be mindful to how you talk to employees, co-workers, friends, neighbors, customers, and especially your family members. Words are very powerful. The words you speak to another person can change a person's mood or attitude in a split second.

> **People with sharp tongues are often oblivious to how they come across to other people.**

While I was in college I worked at Target. One evening I was walking out the door when the new manager, who was walking out the same time, stopped me and asked my name. As a 19-year-old, still pimply-faced, low-self-confidence kid, I was concerned I had done something wrong. I will never forget what he said and how he made me feel:

He crossed his arms, then lifted one arm and pointed his finger at me and said, "If every employee in this store worked as hard as you, I'd have the best Target in the nation." I remember smiling from ear to ear and walking out of that store wanting to scream as loud as I could to the world, "I WORK AT TARGET!" I'm pretty sure the next day, I did circles around everyone and accomplished even more than usual. You can fuel other people by using words of appreciation that show you value them.

The Hurting Zombie:

While working at the hospital, I also worked a part-time job for a small company. Sometimes I went in without any pay just to make sure I was caught up and everything was neat and tidy. One Saturday morning, I was working in different parts of the building when the boss shows up. I thought maybe I would get brownie points for coming in on my day off, but the boss came in and didn't say a whole lot. She walked through the building and then came back. Standing in the doorway, she motioned me over to the door with her finger. Thinking that was a little odd, I went over to her and then she did something odder. She took me by the hand, then took one finger and proceeded to have me shut the light switch off and then on with her hand over mine. Again, I thought this was a little odd. But then what she said took me by surprise. "If you had to pay the light bill, you would know how to turn a light switch off." In the awkward silence she left, and I went home in tears and my enthusiasm for that job went out the window.

As I said before, my self-confidence at that age was not very high. If it happened today, I'd have to be careful! My sassy self may have said, "Lighten up, lady! And no pun intended!" If I left on too many lights in all the rooms I was working in and out of, I think there was definitely a better way it could have been handled.

In looking back, I can see she was hurting because the business was sinking, and she was having difficulty paying the bills. It's true that hurting people hurt other people and hurting people overreact. Unfortunately, on that day, I was the dog that got kicked. Even though it took a while to get my enthusiasm back and work through the emotions of the incident, I made the decision that I would forgive her for her actions. Remember to always look beneath the surface when people don't treat you well. (I'll talk more about reacting to zombies soon.)

The Baby Zombie:

Essentially Baby Zombies are the self-centered people who always want to get their own way. Of course, all of us want to do things our way. The difference is what happens if we do *not* get our own way. Baby Zombies become cry-babies; they whine about everything. They are the non-stop complainers, frowning face-makers, and annoying eye-rollers. Remember when you were a kid and your parents told you to do a certain chore you just hated to do? You put it off, complained, whined, and finally figured out you might as well do it. Well, Baby Zombies continue to procrastinate and whine about their workload, even into adulthood. They have no motivation or interest other than sustaining their own existence.

Honestly, I think the Baby Zombie is the root problem of all zombies, because it stems from selfishness. Selfishness and thinking entirely of oneself is why a person "gets his nose bent out of shape." This results in a bad attitude, moping, biting with words, being mean, or being unnecessarily argumentative for no good reason. Personally, their attitudes stink like their dirty diapers. Baby Zombies in the workplace need to get rid of their pacifiers and grow up.

The Negative Zombie:

We're now to the workplace zombie that everyone has encountered at one time or another. These are the people who NEVER have anything positive to say. Of course, we all complain from time to time, but some people have a default button which opens the spigot of negativity every time they open their mouths.

While at a restaurant, I saw a prominent businessman in town and began some small chit-chat. He commented on the new Hobby Lobby store that was under construction in our small town, saying, "I can't believe they're bringing in a Hobby Lobby. Surely there aren't that many people in this town who do crafts." First, the guy apparently has never been in a Hobby Lobby (he would know it contains more than crafts), and second, our city really needed new businesses to come in and help revive the economy. You would think the guy would be jumping up and down as a businessman that it would bring people and jobs into our city. After the Hobby Lobby opened, one of the managers told me they were breaking records for sales in a community our size!

Two months later, this very same Negative Zombie showed up again at the same restaurant. I decided to start the conversation on a positive note and said, "I hear there's a new indoor mini-golf course with a dinosaur theme coming to our local mall." His response was, "Those people should just pack up their bags and leave town now." To this I immediately responded, "Why would I want to do that—since I'm the owner?" After he floundered a bit, I helped him out by changing the subject.

This zombie resembles the Dream Killer Zombie, which is coming up shortly. The Tee-Rex Mini Golf was my husband's idea for several years, and is doing well! By the way, my husband didn't go to college all those years to be a putt-putt guy. He's a college philosophy teacher by day—who just likes dinosaurs.

Some people live and breathe negativity; it just seems to come naturally to them. They remind me of Pigpen from the Peanuts cartoon, with a cloud hovering around them; or even better, they remind me of the character Joe Btfsplk from Li'l Abner, with a black cloud always over his head. When these people enter the room, you know what to expect from them. At a concert recently, I saw a familiar face on the way out. We both shared that we enjoyed the concert immensely, but

I knew it was coming; she had to find one thing negative and focus on it: "Why can't this city bring in more entertainment like this? I don't know what the problem is with this town." I wanted to give her a Zombie glare and then say, "What do you think they just did?" Instead, I just let her continue for a while and changed the subject when I could.

Negative people can be very sarcastic. Many perpetually negative people, when asked how their days are going, will say things like, "Just peachy" or "Living the dream," when you know they aren't. Their comments charge the air with negativity from the beginning of a conversation; even before your interaction begins, you have to deal with the attitude on display. Negative-minded people can be very draining.

In most cases, people who are negative have had negative circumstances shape their minds. Some people who exude negativity have bad attitudes because of poor choices they have made in their lives. Now they live with the consequences of those poor choices or decisions. Unfortunately, they are in a Catch-22 situation: They're so negative because they are stuck where they are in life, and they are stuck where they are in life because they're so negative. They're between a rock and a hard place. However, despite being "stuck," they choose to remain as they are because they don't want to get out of their comfort zone. Their tunnel vision can't see any way out, yet they don't want to change. Or perhaps they've lived in that "stuck" for so long they stay there because it would take too much energy to get out of it. They would like to see their circumstances change, but do not want to work at the change in themselves it would take to change their circumstances.

These people must live miserable lives! And ultimately, this negativity will affect their health as well (see the later chapter "Attitude and Your Health").

> Some people who exude negativity have bad attitudes because of poor choices they have made in their lives.

The Fearful Zombie:

Kinemortophobia is the fear of zombies, or sometimes the fear of turning into a zombie. It's probably not an issue you have to deal with unless you are obsessed with watching zombies on a screen on a consistent basis. Common fears in life range from claustrophobia (fear of enclosed spaces), arachnophobia (fear of spiders), ophidiophobia (fear of snakes) to ridiculous fears such as nomophobia (fear of being without cell phones), and hippopotomonstrosesquippedaliophobia (fear of long words). If you do a Google search, you'd be amazed by the hundreds of phobias that scare people.

Fearful Zombies find many of their fears in the workplace. They fear losing their jobs, being moved into an unfamiliar position or a position they don't want, or new software and upgrades; they fear rejection, failure, criticism, their bosses, or simply other people. They fear losing control, their jobs being outsourced, or the unknown future. A common workplace fear is metathesiophobia, which is the fear of CHANGE. We are all creatures of habit and we don't like to get out of our comfort zones. As Mark Twain said, "The only person who likes change is a wet baby."

I can't say that I get all excited about change unless the change benefits me. I remember when my wonderful doctor retired, my hair dresser retired, the massage therapist I liked changed occupations, and my first child left home, which all occurred in a one-month span. It was a little dispiriting to start all over to find others to replace these top-notch people (except for my son, who didn't need replaced). Change can be difficult.

Years ago, I woke up and was getting ready for the day when I looked in the mirror while brushing my teeth. I was puzzled by something hanging off my chin. As I got the X10 magnification mirror out to look, it was a long hair. Grossed out by it, I took the tweezers and plucked it, wondering how many people I had already encountered with this billy-goat hair hanging off my chin. A week later, I found it had returned with a buddy on the other side of my chin. After plucking them, I thought about the hot flashes that were occurring more and more, and I put two and two together. I realized I was going through the dreaded "change." When I was younger, I thought only old women went through that change thing. I was only 45 at the time, so I decided my definition of "old" had to be way off.

Now men, as for you—look at your high school yearbook senior picture and compare it to what you saw in the mirror this morning. You would definitely see change (some of you are going to see more dramatic changes than others). Change is inevitable in every area of life! But let's go back to change in the workplace.

Have you ever heard someone say after news of a change, "But we've always done it this way"? When you have a change, you have no control over, i.e., new policies, new standards, new procedures, new boss or co-workers, etc., it's important to collaborate with your team, get positive support from each other, and focus on the benefits of any change. Supporting and encouraging one another during change is vitally important.

If your fears drive you to become a Negative, Baby, or Angry Zombie over the change, you're just hurting yourself. You will also expend more energy fighting the change versus finding the best way to work through the change. Be at peace! Instead of dragging yourself to work and becoming a Biting Zombie by bashing those who made the changes, buck up and just work through it. I know it's easier said than done. Sometimes you just want to scream when something goes against what you've always done. It's also hard when someone tells you what to do when you don't want to do it. I liken it to taking your fingernails and running them down a chalkboard.

While working at a hospital for so many years, I saw many changes. We had simple changes, such as transitioning out of using big bulky typewriters to the large bulky computers, to now laptops or PCs with flat screens. We also had numerous changes in leadership, policies, construction, turnover, etc. We also had huge changes, such as the hospital going from non-profit to profit. Positions were deleted; people were let go. You could feel the stress and see it on the employees' faces every time you walked into the building. Change truly can create fear in people. However, it's been several years now since that transition. People have adapted and you see more smiles.

When you're frustrated with change in the workplace, it's easy to get distracted from what you're supposed to be doing on your job. It's easy to drag yourself through work like a zombie, moaning, groaning, and murmuring. But remember: You're just wasting your energy and time.

With all that said, it remains true that the success of change in any business or organization rests on the leadership. John C. Maxwell, considered the number one leadership expert in the world today, says, "Everything rises and falls on leadership." To make successful changes in the workplace, leaders must be there rooting for the staff and encouraging them, and, more than any other time, being present with and for the staff.

According to David Rock, author of the *Handbook of Neuroleadership*, "Uncertainty registers as an error, gap, or tension in the brain: something that must be corrected before one can feel comfortable again. That is why people crave certainty. Not knowing what will happen next can be profoundly debilitating because it requires extra neural energy. This can diminish memory, undermine performance, and disengage people from the present."

"Change is inevitable in organizations, and when it happens, leadership often underestimates the impact those changes have on employees," said David W. Ballard, Assistant Executive Director for Organizational Excellence with the American Psychological Association Center. "If they damage their relationship with employees, ratcheting up stress levels and creating a climate of negativity and cynicism in the process, managers can wind up undermining the very change efforts they're trying to promote."

Fear can paralyze a person. I remember my first speaking event at an international conference. I didn't feel confident, and when I got up to the stage to speak, I literally froze up. Nothing came out of my mouth—not a single word. Change can trigger fear in employees to the point that they have no mobility. They don't move quickly and can't adjust to changes. This reminds me of a zombie: they're slow-moving and very unproductive.

You can avoid the Fearful Zombie in the workplace during change if you create a plan of action. "Leadership is about not only leading, but implementing change," says Lisa Quast, *Forbes* contributing author. "Prior to making changes that will affect others, it's important for managers to carefully think through: 1) what the specific changes include, 2) who the changes will impact, 3) how it will impact them, and 4) how they might react (understanding reasons why people might resist the changes). Knowing this information makes it easier to create a plan of action for a smooth implementation of the changes."

Change can bring new ideas, opportunities, and new life into an organization. Don't fear it, but embrace it. If you focus on how you can help others through the change, you will make it through the change yourself in much better style.

The Rude Zombie:

The word "rude" means to be offensively impolite or ill-mannered. People are rude for different reasons. I think people can be rude because they are impatient or lack values and character, maybe without knowing it. Sometimes people can be deliberately rude because they don't value others.

When I worked at the hospital, making daily rounds and visiting patients, there was one physician in particular who would come in the room and start talking to the patient while I was still there, as though I weren't even in the room. Normally, physicians would let me finish a sentence, or I would stop and say, "I'll step outside and be right back." But this particular physician was not only rude—he would never even like to make eye contact with me. The first time it happened I was befuddled by his actions. When it happened frequently, I decided his rude actions wouldn't ruin my day; I just understood that was the way he was. He could learn a thing or two from the other courteous and kind physicians with which I worked. Fortunately, he no longer works at that hospital.

As mentioned in the Negative Zombie portion, my husband and I own a mini-golf course. During the summer it's been a great place for our kids to work. One night a father and his five teens came in. He asked my son, Nathan, if they could have a discount since there were six of them and he didn't want to pay five dollars apiece to play golf. Nathan replied that kids two years old and under were free, but not older kids. The father looked at all his kids, looked at Nathan and said, "Well, they're all two years old." Nathan replied, "Sorry, no discount." The father then looked at his kids and said, "What do we say?" and they all in unison turned to my son and loudly yelled, "Boo!" Then they turned around and walked out.

When Nathan came home and told us about this incident, my husband and I just looked at him with our mouths open. We couldn't even imagine training our children to be rude to people who were just doing their jobs. It is sadly true that some people are rude because of their upbringing.

Unfortunately, some parents don't teach their children rules and manners. And the children become Rude Zombies!

The Constipated Zombie:

This may seem a bit blunt, but here goes: Did you know if you're constipated you will be in a bad mood? This question always catches people off guard. However, think about it: If your plumbing's not working, then you're wasting time in the bathroom, lethargic, possibly dealing with stomach cramps, and being grumpy about it. If you don't feel well, you drag yourself into work and your physical feelings zap your energy. Seriously, if constipated, you will be non-productive on the job. (I am not just talking about poor physical feelings; I am being *very specific* about the physical problem.)

Make sure you drink lots of water, eat nuts and raisins, take laxatives and probiotics, eat prunes, and keep other fiber snacks handy to maintain a healthy diet. If you can, go for a walk on your break or lunch time, even if it's only for five minutes. If you eat healthily, you'll feel good if you're moving, if you know what I mean. (I'll talk more about attitude and your health in Chapter 10.)

The Worried Zombie:

"Worry is like a rocking chair. It gives you something to do, but it gets you nowhere," says best-selling author and humorist, Erma Bombeck.

Worried Zombies are the people who always expect bad things to happen, and they make their expectations known. Their mindset is always "What if?" They expect the worst. My mother, whom I love dearly, deals with these troublesome expectations often. On Mother's Day several years ago, I had cooked a nice meal for her and my family. We were enjoying the delicious meal, when all of a sudden, the sky grew dark, the black clouds settled in, and the wind picked up. My mom looked outside and said matter-of-factly, "The roof's going to cave in and we're all going to die!" Since we're still upright, my husband and I still laugh about that to this day.

As was mentioned earlier, you have to look beneath the surface to see why people act the way they do. When people worry incessantly, you need to look beneath the surface again. When my little sister passed away unexpectedly at the young age of 39, it was very devastating to the family. Seeing the grief on my parent's faces was heart-wrenching. I'm sure now, especially with my extensive travel schedule, my mom fears living through that horrific experience of losing a child again. On your job, if you have people who constantly worry, there is probably a root cause. Be patient and loving with those folks. Many Worried Zombies eventually can be cured.

The Complacent Zombie:

While talking with a supervisor of a corporation, I casually asked her what sticks out the most in her mind when I mention negativity in the workplace. She immediately replied, "Complacency." She was referring to employees who she felt had "learned-helplessness." They were no longer engaged with their work; they mindlessly did their jobs, had no initiative, didn't take any risks, lost their passion, and had no hope for a better tomorrow. Their attitudes were "This is the way it is, so why try?" or "No one recognizes the work I've done, so why should I go above and beyond? Why put forth extra effort?" When asked how she dealt with complacency, she said she does her best to offer positive reinforcement on a regular basis.

Unfortunately, the philosophy of some people seems to be, "How little can I do and get by with it? I'm just going to do what I'm hired to do—if that!" It is difficult to see these people becoming very successful on their jobs or in their lives. Highly successful people will go beyond and above expectations. Complacent Zombies can lead to high turnover, lower profits, less innovation, and lack of teamwork.

The Angry Zombie:

Years ago, I was called into the office to speak with my boss. He wanted to know if I was angry. I was shocked that he would ask me that question, and I asked him why he thought that. It turned out that according to several employees, when I walked down the hallway, I looked mad. I laughed and said that I was in deep thought, and he told me to pay attention to my own body language. Although it was a little embarrassing, I was glad that he made me aware of my how I was coming across to people.

On the other hand, there are those people who really *are* mad on the job, who get and stay very angry. Unfortunately, these people are easily angered over small things; they are "those who are given to anger." Don't associate with those who are given to anger! They are like pressure cookers, and you know at any time they could explode. Their blood boils if someone looks at them wrong; they easily get upset over small matters; they scream, swear, and constantly blame others; they are impatient and resentful. They use up so much energy which takes away from the energy they should be exerting on the job and in life.

I've actually seen people throw things, kick things, scream, and yell—which, of course, resulted in them having *great results*. Great results, that is, if what you want is high blood pressure and more wasted energy. Essentially, they waste your energy as well if you have to deal with them or even be around them.

It's important to remember the three C's if you work with an Angry Zombie: Stay cool, calm, and collected. If you don't feel safe, get away from that person. Wait to talk with them until after they have cooled off. I love the wisdom of King Solomon: "A soft answer turns away anger." Your calm demeanor and attitude could change their angry attitudes.

Angry Zombies tend to have a problem with road rage. When visiting my sister in Orlando a few years ago, we were driving among both tourists and the locals, which can be a challenge. My brother-in-law had severe road rage while driving in and out of traffic, honking at people, and using rather strong explicit language to those people (who didn't hear him anyway). Many times, I was clutching the seat and wondering if I would be walking through the Pearly Gates soon (which are not a sub-division of Orlando). Why get in zombie mode on the drive to work before you even start the day? Your blood pressure will be sky-high and your energy for the day will already be expended.

Angry Zombies are usually disgruntled employees. If you find that the Angry Zombies are showing any signs of hostility, then you need to start documenting any unusual behavior and report it to Human Resources or your boss. You need to care about your own well-being and those around you, so keep your composure and walk away from the situation, as some people are impossible to please.

Stay cool, calm, and collected.

Remember that anger is unhealthy. "Anger causes stress and hurts your health," according to Allen Elkin in *Stress Management for Dummies*. The Chinese proverb fits here: "If you are patient in one moment of anger, you will escape a hundred days of sorrow."

The Bully Zombie:

It can be very frustrating and stressful if you work with bullies. They can be customers, co-workers, or your boss. My brother used to work in a prison corrections facility. After being attacked twice and ending up in the emergency room, one day his boss informed him that he was on a prisoners' hit list, then turned around and walked away. It's hard to enjoy a job when you work under those types of circumstances. After twelve years, my brother finally decided to leave and even forgo all benefits for his own sanity and safety.

Bully zombies are essentially just mean people. Some people are obnoxious, but in some being obnoxious takes the form of being just plain old mean. Chances are people in their lives were mean to them, so they have mimicked those traits. Donald L. Hicks sums up how I believe any bully, young or old, is best described: "When someone would mistreat, misinform, misuse, misguide, mishandle, mislead... or any other 'mis'... others, they're obviously 'missing' something from their lives."

According to the WBI (Workplace Bullying Institute), if you are bullied it's because you posed a threat to the bully. "Workplace Bullying is repeated, health-harming mistreatment of one or more persons (the targets) by one or more perpetrators. It is *abusive* conduct that is threatening, humiliating, or intimidating, or work-interference, i.e. sabotage, which prevents work from getting done." Abusive conduct includes verbal abuse. If you are bullied by the Bully Zombie, I urge you to ask for help. You do not have to "stand up to" this type of situation on your own.

I like to recommend the S.K.A.T.E. strategy. S stands for "Say No" to reacting to the bully and choosing not to argue with, fight with, or get infected by him. K stands for "Keep Your Cool." As stated before, stay cool, calm, and collected. A stands for "Ask for Help" from co-workers, your boss, Human Resources, or the police if need be. T stands for "Treat Others Well"—or at least as well as you can in the particular situation. And E stands for "Encourage Others." Many times, a bully threat could have been prevented if you are pro-active, or someone who is being bullied can be encouraged and helped by your support. You never know; you might be the one person who gave the words of encouragement the other needed.

The Argumentative Zombie:

Have you ever met a know-it-all? This is a person who is an expert in *everything* and has always "been there and done that." These are people who delight in making others feel stupid. They also never admit it when they are wrong. Doesn't that drive you nuts! These people are also nit-pickers over the most minute things. They are not good listeners because they are thinking of what they are going to say next to win their argument or to make the other speaker look foolish.

When we go beneath the surface, we usually see that these people are very insecure. When you must deal with these people you have two options: (1) Follow the 101% Principle (find 1% that you can agree on and give it your 100% of your effort). We all have points we don't agree on, but maybe there is *one thing* you can agree on? (2) Or, do a lot of smiling, nodding, and biting your lip, consider the source, and move on.

The Grieving Zombie:

Not all zombies are mean, angry, or deliberately harmful. I used to travel to a large company several times a year and would see one certain employee every time. She was a young lady with whom I got on the elevator with one day. As always, she was quiet, and I felt she needed to notify her face that she had the ability to turn her lips to an upward position. I wondered many times, "What is her problem?" We got off the elevator and I told her to have a nice Christmas holiday. Her reply was, "I never have a nice Christmas holiday." I thought, Oh, boy; you've got the genes of both Mr. Scrooge and the Grinch.

Then my heart sank with what came out of her mouth next. She said, "My parents both died on Christmas in an accident." I was so caught off guard, I froze. But after stepping off the elevator that day, I always looked at this young lady with a different attitude and always tried to give her encouraging words for the day. You never know what people have gone through or are going through. Sometimes people are living as Zombies through no fault of their own.

Grief can paralyze a person. I mentioned it earlier, but I will never forget the day I got home from visiting a Pizza Hut and there were numerous messages from my sister and brother-in-law that I needed to call as soon as possible. I knew something had happened to my other precious sister, Lisa. When they told me she had been found dead on her living room floor, I sank to the ground. I remained there for a time, paralyzed.

Again, when someone has a particular behavior and attitude, you must go beneath the surface. There is a reason why people act the way they do.

The Tired Zombie:

My bad and crabby attitude goes off the meter when I don't get enough sleep. Tired Zombies drag themselves into work. From my own experience, if I don't get enough sleep, I'm very short-fused. If you work with someone who hasn't gotten much sleep, make sure you give that person space; keep your distance. It's vitally important that the coffee pot is working that day! Better yet, have someone run out to Starbucks and get Caramel Macchiato for everyone.

Sometimes co-workers are tired because of exhausting or draining experiences in their lives. Recently a friend spoke about her daughter's business that was flooded and destroyed in Des Moines, Iowa, only ninety minutes from my home. There was close to a million dollars in damage to her business.

I can't even begin to imagine people who have experienced natural tragedies such as flooding, earthquakes, and hurricanes. It is quite easy for them to become Tired Zombies. Lifting these people up in prayer and giving the best support we can during difficult times will help people in the workplace more than you could ever imagine.

The Drama Queen Zombie:

(First, I need to clarify that there are Drama Kings in the workplace just as there are Drama Queens.)

While stopped at a busy intersection a few days ago, I looked in the rear-view mirror to see a woman get out of the passenger's side, slam the door, and stomp off. I wondered what that drama story was all about. It might have been a serious situation, but the "drama" I am talking about is not usually serious at all—except in the Drama Queen Zombie's head! Often "drama" is an attempt to infuse a high level of emotion and excitement into events that are otherwise pretty much commonplace and unimpressive. Voices get raised and tempers flare at minor provocations or life events. Let's face it: *Everyone* has gotten bad service at a restaurant or gotten cut off in traffic, right? *Everyone* has had arguments with significant others or friends. Why make our little irritations the center of everyone else's time and attention?

When you have drama at home, it carries over into the workplace. Often co-workers are tired of hearing the same soap opera day after day. The Drama Queens also stir up drama at work when they should be working. Drama includes gossip via email, Facebook, by the water cooler, or during unproductive meetings. Drama Queens say things like, "I don't think so and so likes me," "I think so and so will get fired," or "Did you hear what I heard?" They are unproductive, to say the least, but they also cause others to become unproductive. Drama Queens are manipulators and trouble-makers; they like to get others tangled up in their little situations. Stay away from them!

"To dramatically improve productivity, you must eliminate time-sucking, whining, negativity, and drama in the workplace," says Laura Stack, best-selling author of *Leave the Office Earlier*.

The Thoughtless Zombie:

If you ever get to meet my daughter, Erin, you will find she's very conscientious, tender-hearted, and hard-working. After graduating from high school, she worked three jobs to prepare for going to college. When she came back home over Christmas break, since she was going to be home for a span of five weeks, she looked for a temporary job. She got hired by a local bakery, but when she got there the first day, the woman training her was harsh and rude. The trainer was very condescending and spent most of the training time complaining about her ailments and her life. Erin enjoyed talking to the people who came in, but did get a little frazzled by this one particular workplace zombie.

One day Erin came home from work and told me that she wanted to tell this complainer, "My Mom speaks on people acting like zombies and you need to go to one of her classes." Of course, she's very kind-hearted and would never do that.

> In this life, you will unfortunately encounter people who act like they don't have any brains in their heads.

A few weeks later, on Christmas Eve, Erin came downstairs with her phone to show me a text that she had received from the manager that Erin was fired due to lack of business.

First of all, Mama Bear was ready to march right down there and let the manager know how unprofessional it was to fire someone through a text, let alone on Christmas Eve. But I chose not to go into zombie mode.

Have you ever run into people about whom you think, "You've got to be kidding! Everybody knows that!" Apparently, this boss was thoughtless on the way to let an employee go and what day of the week it was.

In this life, you will unfortunately encounter people who act like they don't have any brains in their heads. Often, as in this case, you might not be able to do anything about it. Just learn to expect "brainless" situations and continue past them.

The Entitled Zombie:

When I mention Entitled Zombies, you may think I'm going to talk about millennials, since many point out their sense of "entitlement." However, quite the contrary. Since I've worked with all social-economic levels of people and been exposed to a large number of different industries, businesses, cultures, and organizations during the last several years, I've come to a conclusion. There have always been and will always be people who feel entitled. The Rude Zombie I mentioned earlier who wanted all of his "two-year-olds" to get in free to play mini-golf was also an entitled zombie—but he was definitely not a millennial.

Recently I was speaking to my friend, Teri, who owns a high-end consignment shop. She was telling me about a group of people who came in on several occasions, piled loads of shoes and clothes on the counter, and demanded the price be cut by 75%. After an exhausting amount of time with them and being firm with the group and letting them know she valued her consigners, they either walked out (leaving a mess) or went ahead and bought the items at the regular price. She cringes every time they walk into the store. She then said that the group was at a church garage sale and said they wanted the whole table of jeans for $25. All the jeans were valued at $150. The lady who was running the sale said no, as the money was going to a ministry project and they had just opened the sale. The man wanting them for practically nothing saw a large garbage bag under the table and started loading the bag up. He walked over to her, lay down $25, and started walking out. Some of the people detained him and the lady called the police. Unfortunately, the police could not arrest him for robbery. They said by laying down the money, he made a transaction, and they couldn't do anything about it. That doesn't make sense to me, but my point is that people of all ages demand entitlement.

Going back to the stereotype of millennials and entitlement in the workplace, I'm sure there is a percentage of them that do feel entitled. Perhaps they'll read this book, or you can buy them a copy. We all need to learn the best remedies to reduce entitlement are, first, to teach people the importance of gratitude for what they do receive, and second, to teach humility in receiving the graciousness of others. Having raised millennials of my own assures me that not all millennials feel entitled.

The Social Media Zombie:

Social media certainly affects people's attitudes and behavior. How many times have you seen someone post their luxurious vacation—and suddenly the green eye of jealousy and envy pops up on your own screen of negativity? Or how many of you remember the recent Rosanne Barr Show being cancelled due to Rosanne's racist tweet? Would she have made that comment to Valerie Jarrett's face? Okay, maybe she would have. But the point is, social media transforms the way we communicate. I've seen people turn into zombies on Facebook, fighting over politics, religion, or any other topic raised. People seem much more inclined to say something stupid when it is spoken through a computer screen instead of face to face.

One night I was performing magic in a restaurant and a group of what I thought were college students came in all together—about five of them. While they were waiting for the host to seat them, the one male in the group said, "Let's all go to the restroom." He herded the females down toward the restroom. Now first of all, it's very rare for a guy to say that, and then what are the odds that all five needed to go at the same time? Anyway, they all went to the restroom. About two minutes later, I looked up to see two of them pushing each other back and forth out on the restaurant floor. I thought they were just horse-playing. But as I kept watching it unfold, I saw that the guy was beating up one of the waitresses. The next thing I knew, the others in the group surrounded the waitress, pulling her hair and kicking her. Then the managers saw what was happening, rushed over, and started yelling at them to stop. The five fled out of the restaurant. It all happened so quickly, nothing else was done; no one else had a chance to interfere. The police came, the other staff and I were interviewed, and I was a little shaken up when I left.

Maybe I have lived a sheltered life, as I have never seen anyone get the pulp beaten out of them. After that night, I had trouble going to sleep. When I was out in public at night, I kept looking over my shoulder, concerned I would see that gang again.

Now I am telling you that story just to explain how it all began. The waitress who was beaten up had earlier posted on Facebook, "You ugly" [sic] to some girl who apparently wasn't her BFF. The non-BFF didn't like the posting, so she had her group of thugs go into the public restaurant to show the waitress a thing or two. Herds of Zombies can even emerge from social media!

That sort of scenario is quite rare, but there definitely is a more common type of Social Media Zombie. Through the years I've been hired for a large variety of venues. However, no matter where I'm at, it's interesting to see people pull out their phones in company, while working, or while engaged (supposedly) in some other activity, as if no one is looking, so they can check their latest status, likes, and news. According to a CNBC news blog by Mark Fahey, "Time wasted on Facebook could be costing employers trillions in lost productivity." My question to you: How often do you sneak a peek while on the job? Can you imagine even spending an hour or two without checking social media? If not, you may have social media zombie tendencies.

It's very tempting to try to see and hear the latest. I highly recommend taking 24 hours or even a whole week to live without social media. See how much more productive your life is!

Defeated Zombie:

Often our attitudes go sour when we don't see our dreams fulfilled. I love the title of John Maxwell's book, *Sometimes You Win, Sometimes You Learn*. I wish I would have read that book when I was a teen. I ran track in school, and when I didn't cut my time or win a race, I was demoralized for days and my attitude showed it. Through the years, when I would fail at anything I attempted, I considered myself a loser and a failure.

Through history, you will find people who have failed but they were determined, persistent, and didn't give up. Walt Disney was told he had no imagination. It was reported that Stephen Spielberg was rejected by both the USC and UCLA, at least once each, for his low grades on a transcript. Those are just a few people who could have let failure dominate their lives, but they chose not to be defeated.

The Dream-Killing Zombie:

When you have a dream in your heart to do something extraordinary, not everyone jumps on board, understands, or buys into your vision. Years ago, when I told my husband I was going to become a professional clown, he told me he really didn't like clowns. His exact words regarding clowns: They were "alcoholics who couldn't get real jobs." Of course, after time, his belief that a clown was a scary alcoholic bum changed after my professional training in the art of clowning and he saw my success. I got to travel around the world on Royal Caribbean Cruise Lines, guest perform with Ringling Brothers and Barnum and Bailey Circus, guest perform with the Carden International Circus, receive first place at the World Clown Convention, have my clown character, "Dizzy," painted by international artist, P. Buckley Moss, and have my character molded into electric lights at our city's Christmas Holiday Nights in Lights drive-through event. More importantly, I was able to influence thousands of kids through the years with character-building programs in schools as well as touch countless patients through my humor therapy program at the hospital. All of this changed his attitude toward me as a performing clown (although for him the jury is still out for *other* clowns). To this day I still have cancer survivors stop me and tell me they remembered their first day of chemo and the red nose I gave them. My husband has become my biggest fan.

Twenty years later when I told my husband I was going to be a motivational speaker, he said, "I hate motivational speakers." Unfortunately, his experience with motivational speakers was similar to that of watching someone like the fictional character Matt Foley (portrayed by Chris Farley), the motivational speaker. My husband thought of motivational speakers as people who tried to "pump people up" with hot air instead of substance.

There were others who said things like, "Nobody in town will hire you as a speaker because they think you're just a clown." Others said, "Why would you change your career?" Remember what I said earlier: "What you're doing today is always preparing you for what you're going to do tomorrow." With my experience as a family entertainer, professional clown, magician, and expert in laughter, it has given me a great platform to speak. And yes, I've been hired in my hometown numerous times to speak with great success.

I remember a season of life when I felt "stuck." Ever been there before? During that time, I was attending a magician's conference and the keynote speaker did an illusion and said something that resonated with me. It gave me hope and a new perspective. It lit a fire on the inside of me. I remember sitting there with my mouth wide open in astonishment and I said to myself, "That's what I want to do someday. I want to be able to inspire people when they're stuck." When you know God has put a desire and dream in your heart, you have to ignore the Zombie Dream Killers' attitudes and keep pressing on. As for my husband, he's been to many of my speaking engagements, and he loves the speaker!

Many times, people will try to kill your dreams because they don't understand what you want to do, they have opinions on what's best for you, they're jealous, or they fear what you do will

What you're doing today is always preparing you for what you're going to do tomorrow.

diminish them in some way. In the workplace, when you have a great idea, don't throw it away if the Dream Killer Zombies try to kill those ideas. Don't let them extinguish your inner flame. Stay focused and press on!

The Stressed Zombie:

When your co-workers have a bad attitude and snap at you, it is often due to stress. Because I think stress affects attitudes greatly (this I say from experience), I've written a whole chapter on stress and its effects on your attitude (Chapter 9). There I will not only talk about the consequences of stress, but give you a strategy to minimize, eliminate, or manage the stress in your life.

I want to give you a strategy on how to survive working with the living dead. But first, want to address the living dead who might be criminals, clients, or customers.

Criminals, Clients, and Customers Who Act Like Zombies

Darryl Rivers is a former police officer and hostage negotiator. He heads up TheLeadCompany.net, a communications, human behaviors, and leadership training company. I asked him for his perspective on negativity and dealing with criminals. Here is Darryl's response:

> Attitudes and beliefs are truly contagious, whether positive or negative. This truth is amplified when working in a close-knit group or community such as law enforcement or any other type of first responder. There is an entry phase that the new officer goes through; this phase will help a young officer's professional perception, giving him or her a "new set of glasses" from which to view the planet.
>
> We all know people do not call 911 because they are experiencing the best day of their life. Therefore, the modern officer gets to encounter society at its emotional climax of fear, anger, frustration, despair, loss, confusion, helplessness, and many other emotional responses that can be triggered from emergencies, physical harm, or mental

trauma. As a retired law enforcement professional, I recognized there was a high level of empathy during my initial year or so as a police officer. Then it happens; our brains begin to set up coping mechanisms. The more tragic situations I was exposed to, the more desensitized I became to the unfortunate plight of the community I served. Of course, there are the certain situations for which you will always have compassion, such as crimes against women and children for most male officers, and crimes of a sexual nature for female officers. As a young officer, I had no idea what an anchor was or could do for my personal and professional stability. What seemed to be the most important moments in the lives of those I encountered were routine moments for me, due to the constant exposure of these extremes. When a thing becomes a constant, it becomes normal. Normal is not special, yet I was expected to treat every case as special. This is the beginning stage of cynicism. Then it happened! My partner and friend was killed in the line of duty. My perspective changed immediately. Sometimes officers have a sense of invincibility when they are the answer to the calamity of the world. That sense of invincibility eroded quickly. Officer Steward became my anchor—a reminder that real people hurt and hurt does not discriminate. I felt very human, vulnerable, and once again empathetic toward everyone I encountered. This tragic loss was the anchoring factor that was responsible for the resurgence of my positive attitude.

So let's talk about the effects of attitude in the law enforcement profession. I am convinced no one can make anyone anything. We can influence certain things, but if you squeeze a sponge, whatever is in it comes out. You did not make it full of water; you just exposed the reality that it was full of water by applying pressure. When I realized no one can make me mad, I also realized the only reason I became mad was because mad was already in me. No one made me become what I already was. We all collect experiences and tell ourselves how to categorize them. We can soak up lots of things in our daily task. Most of what we soak up is from other officers and their attitudes, perceptions, and altered world view. This is why an anchor that keeps you grounded to your positive attitude is so important. Being the positive that constantly encounters negatives is something special. This makes it a lot easier to treat each case as special.

To make positivity louder, we have to make positivity more contagious. Being an anchor of positivity in law enforcement can be a very challenging task. I have experienced the rewards of this challenge. The most important reward was the one of personal peace in the midst of chaos. A healthy mind and a healthy attitude go hand in hand. It's a daunting task to obtain professional peace while being void of personal peace. Professional peace translates to maximum effort when all appears to be lost. Professional peace eliminates burn-out syndrome. Professional peace magnifies professional pride and tenacity. Professional peace is contagious! Your attitude is the springboard to personal and professional excellence. If you don't feel good about it… you won't be excellent at it.

I recently had the pleasure of talking to a police officer by the name of Alex, from Oskaloosa, Iowa. I asked him how he kept his attitude in check when dealing with criminals. He said he focused on talking with anybody he dealt with on his job with respect. He said he had to be intentional about not raising his voice to them, and speaking in a calm voice, which many times determined the outcome. If he yells when they're yelling, the problem just escalates. Many times, he found that when he would speak with respect they would back off. On the flipside, it's very difficult and stressful when a criminal is screaming and calling you every word in the book. He stated that he's not in the field like he used to be, as he needed to make a change due to the high stress. As I said earlier, it's important to take time to reflect and decide if it's time to make a change in your work life.

Many of you may not work with criminals, but you do work with clients or customers who act like zombies and at times want to bite your head off. It can be very difficult to have a positive attitude when they speak ugly, act stupid, or don't agree with your policies. I rarely ever have to work at our Tee-Rex Mini Golf, but as a co-owner with my husband, I was glad one night when I filled in for someone. I gained a new perspective when five people in their twenties came in and used foul language throughout the course and began posing for obscene photos. There are times you have to be firm and hold your ground with unruly people. When I left, my stress level was high and attitude was in the balance. As I mentioned before, I have a whole chapter on stress and attitude and will give you a strategy on how to manage that stress later.

What about the customers who complain? When I was a Patient Representative/Advocate years ago, my primary job was to handle all patient complaints. I enjoyed it immensely, but there were days when the patient was complaining for no good reason. Is the customer or client always right? Some well-known companies claim to say yes, but I say no. It boils down to perspective and how you handle each particular situation. When a customer, patient, or client complains or growls at you, it's vitally important to remember two words. While looking in the customer's eyes as they vent, repeat these two words mentally over and over again until it's time to open your mouth. Those two words are self-control and professionalism. Self-control and professionalism. Self-control and professionalism. If you do that, it will save you from lots of heartache and trouble and keep you steered in the problem-solving direction.

There have been thousands of books written on customer service, so I would like to recommend two that would be beneficial if you want to do a deeper dive into actual phrases to use for different customer service circumstances. Both books are by Robert Bacal: *Perfect Phrases for Customer Service* and *If it Wasn't for the Customer, I'd Really Like This Job.*

Whether it's workplace zombies you work for or those you serve, I now want to give you strategies on how to survive among them.

PART 2

CAN YOU SURVIVE AMONG THE LIVING DEAD?

CHAPTER 3

ADJUST TO NEGATIVE PEOPLE

Do you want a strategy that works?

"The last of human freedoms is to choose one's attitude in
any given set of circumstances, to choose one's own way."

—Victor Frankl, Holocaust Survivor

So what should you do when you see a workplace zombie?
Should you pull out your sharpest weapon, as they do on
television, and hide behind the door? Definitely not!

Here's an idea which could increase revenue in hospitals
and clinics with mind-blowing results. They could open a
department called "Zombie Health." People with any of the
negative traits previously listed would go in for an inocula-
tion. The line would be long, so nurses would just line them
up in the hallways. The "sweetness serum" would be injected,
and the cured zombies would walk out being sweet nice people from then on.

Okay, so maybe that's a little too far. That scenario would
never take place. Therefore, I want to give you five different
strategies on how to deal with the living dead. Depending on
the situation, you might have to use one, some, or all of them.

#1 DON'T GO TO THEIR GRAVE

In other words, don't descend to their level. Basically, that's what a negative person wants you to do, because misery loves company and negativity breeds negativity. They don't want to be the only ones griping, complaining, whining, bashing the boss, back-biting co-workers, or having a pity party. If you get sucked in, they will squeeze the life out of you; then you will be dragging yourself around as they are.

I want to make it clear that I'm not talking about the person who occasionally complains or vents. You must be very sensitive to know when to listen and when to walk away. Some people do have legitimate problems or concerns. You don't want to be heartless and not help when there is a definite need. However, I think you will be able to spot the type of people I'm referring to. I'm talking about the people who are so negative for no good reasons, and who will not change even if something good is staring them in the face.

As I mentioned before, my brother was a guard in a correctional facility and prison. He dealt with many violent, foul-mouthed, and mean people. I know many times he had to bite his lip when they had lipped off to him. It takes self-discipline not to descend to these people's level.

#2 UNDERSTAND THAT EVERYONE FUNCTIONS DIFFERENTLY

I used to get so frustrated with people who didn't operate the way I did. It was years before I understood that you must communicate with people differently and have different expectations of people who don't have the psychological or genetic make-up you do. On the well-known DISC personality profile chart, I'm a very high D (Confident, competitive, emphasis on accomplishment and results, highly motivated). It's probably good I married someone who is the opposite, which is a high S (Steady, slow, and stable). My husband occasionally pulls the reins back on me every now and then.

It's taken some time, but now my expectations of others have changed, I'm more patient with people, and I try to go with the flow. If you understand that people don't operate the way you do, you'll give them more space, be more forgiving, and exercise greater patience with them.

Teddy Roosevelt said, "The most important single ingredient in the formula for success is knowing how to get along with people." I think that sums it up.

#3 STAY AWAY, HIDE, OR DISTANCE YOURSELF FROM THEM

How many times has this happened to you? You go into the grocery store focusing on whether to grill hamburgers or make tacos, when suddenly you see the living dead dragging themselves through the store. It's the person from work who wants to talk incessantly about his or her complaints with the boss, co-workers, or workload. You quickly swerve your cart over to aisle eight and begin studying the back of a bag of dog food—and you don't even own a dog. Out of the corner of your eye you see him again and make your way to the front check-out, deciding you're going to order pizza for dinner.

I'm not saying we should be snooty in our dealings with others; I just believe your time is valuable. Why let someone waste your time and energy when you know from experience you cannot help him or her? You've heard of secondhand smoke. Secondhand smoke causes numerous health problems to people who inhale smoke involuntarily. Well, secondhand negativity can also be inhaled by people involuntarily and cause numerous emotional problems. When you're at work and sitting next to people like this, I'm sure it would be obvious if you started wearing ear plugs or mega-sized ear phones. When possible, politely change the subject, honestly tell someone you need to get something finished, or maybe try to move to another area. During break time you may need to go for a healthy walk or simply shift locations for a while. Do what you can to take a break from these workplace zombies. Don't be drawn into negative discussions.

#4 BE AS GRACIOUS AS POSSIBLE

Sometimes you have to kill problems with kindness. For ten years my husband and I had been house shopping. One day we pulled into the driveway of our dream house. We got out and fell in love with this house. We called our best friends, who lived a block away, to come over and see it. They walked around it with us. We peeked in the windows (it was empty); they asked us if we were going to buy it. We laughed and told them no, we couldn't afford it at this stage of our life; it was just a dream house. We thought it would be fun to look at it anyway.

After the realtor showed it to all of us, our friends asked us several times again over the next few days if we were going to buy it, and we said no. A few weeks later, our friends bought MY HOUSE! I turned into a zombie before the day was over. My rotten attitude was obvious, as I was upset that they bought OUR house. In reality, of course, it wasn't our house at all. Our friends even had told us they were interested in the house as well and thinking about buying it if we weren't. Still, the sting of my feelings was there. After I struggled with this over the next couple of weeks, I decided that there was a better house out there waiting for us and we would buy it at the right time.

So what kindness could I show to them? I went out and bought a house-warming gift that I would want someone to buy me and took it to THEIR new home. It's very important to take action steps to help you overcome a zombie attitude. Your emotions and feelings will line up if you first take steps to change your attitude. Remember, it's a CHOICE and you make it.

My hairdresser is also a dental assistant (so she can brush just about anything). However, she recently left her dental job because the boss was not only demanding, but non-caring, rigid, sharp with her words, and downright mean. Staci, who is about the sweetest thing you ever met, needed to have her previous boss sign a form that she was no longer working at that dental practice. Staci took the paper to her and she refused to sign it. It would take maybe three seconds, but she wanted to make the process difficult. When Staci went home, she was very aggravated with the woman. She remembered reading a proverb which said, "If your enemy is hungry, give him food to eat." She decided to make her a pan of delicious brownies and then took the warm brownies to her. She had decided she didn't want to become infected by this zombie boss, so she decided to kill the zombie with kindness and be gracious to her. By the way, she chose not to add a secret ingredient like Minny did when she baked a pie for Hilly as seen in the movie *The Help*. (You'd understand if you saw the movie.)

An employee who used to work for me didn't show up for work one day. I called her and asked if there was a problem. She was short with me and gave me a lame excuse, so I reminded her

> **It's very important to take action steps to help you overcome a zombie attitude.**

how important it was to let me know if she couldn't work so that I could replace her. She said she would, and I didn't think about it again until a few days later. I was called into *my* boss's office because the employee called him and said that I was mean to her. Oh, brother! Boggled by her accusations, I decided to kill her with kindness by getting her a gift.

I knew she also worked another part-time job thirty minutes away, so I purchased a nice gift and drove it over to her.

She was a receptionist and when I walked in and set it on her desk, her eyes got as big as saucers. I told her I wanted her to have a good day. Interestingly enough, she never showed back up for work again and quit. I think she had issues.

When I was teaching this topic at a conference, at the end of the session, a gentleman commented that he and those at his table discussed that they could not do this with certain individuals that they worked with. I replied, "I didn't say it was an easy thing to do." Looking back, I was probably gritting my teeth when I paid for the gift, took the time to drive it over to her, and looked her in the eyes. But when I left, I knew that I was not infected with the zombie virus. I knew that I had the choice to be consumed with her spiteful attitude or an attitude of joy. There is something about giving to others that will build you into a better person. Plus, you never know what might happen due to your act of kindness; maybe that person will think to do likewise to someone else down the road. Or maybe people will think about what they did to you and realize they were wrong. Or maybe they're like you and me, people who sometimes go through seasons of life that are rough and bumpy, hoping for someone to take the time to share kindness.

There will be times in life when you get thrown under the bus—people won't talk to you or treat you well. It's important to intentionally take action steps to help other people's negative attitudes and actions NOT show up in you. Remember to be gracious.

#5 INFECT PEOPLE WITH YOUR POSITIVE ATTITUDE

Just as Zombie attitudes can be infectious, so also are the good. Honestly, I think the best way to deal with the living dead is to infect *them* with your enthusiasm and positive attitude. Be a Steady Eddy; remain cool, calm, and collected when negative situations arise. This book is primarily about zombies in the workplace, but I feel strongly that your personal life affects your professional life and your professional life affects your personal life. You can take your attitude from home to work, affecting your productivity, and vice versa.

Let's talk about the immediate family and close relatives who act like the living dead. You can't alienate yourself from your actual family. If you live in a negative atmosphere, then I advise you to talk to the family member involved. Under the negativity there is usually an underlying issue. It is important to address it, possibly even to the extent of receiving professional help. With all family members, you may have to hold your tongue so that the zombie doesn't get stirred up either in you or in them.

The bottom line is you need to LOVE those around you. In the long run, that may be what they need the most. If you remain a rock to them, they will turn to you for help. Think to yourself—how can I improve this situation? Focus on solutions even when you have the feeling, "This person will never change."

I have said that you should infect others with your enthusiasm and positive spirit. However, before I conclude this, I also need to say that life is not all rainbows, unicorns, and singing. There are times when you get in a slump or a funk. You may go through some type of tribulation or what I call a season of stress. I'm a pretty upbeat type of person and usually very positive, but let me tell you about the day I went to visit my chiropractor, Dr. Cosgrove. I had bummed up my neck, shoulder, ribs, hip, and ankles. I don't remember exactly how the conversation went, but I was hurting and, apparently, a cloud of negativity was rapidly forming around me. I was rattling on and on about negative situations in a negative manner.

Finally, during the adjustment period, Dr. Cosgrove said, "Can you tell me something positive?" I said, "In regard to what?" He replied, "I want to get you out of this mode that you're in; let's talk about something positive."

It caught me off guard, but did me good at the same time. It immediately showed me 1) that I had slipped into the living-dead mode without realizing it, and 2) what a great way to turn a negative conversation around. Negativity is toxic and can be contagious. Dr. Cosgrove was probably thinking, "I don't want that negativity to infect me!" I'm so glad that he brought it to my attention and infected me with his positive attitude.

In summary, when you deal with the living dead and their Zombie Attitudes:

> **First, don't go to their grave. Don't let them drag you down to their level.**
> **Second, understand that everyone functions differently.**
> **Third, stay away from them. Hide or distance yourself if necessary.**
> **Fourth, remain as gracious as possible in your dealings with those around you.**
> **Fifth, don't get infected! Rather, you infect others with your positive attitude.**

Remember that you must intentionally take action steps to help you resist infectious negative attitudes.

CHAPTER 4

ENTHUSIASM IS CONTAGIOUS

Can I really laugh at work?

"Success is the ability to go from failure to failure without losing your enthusiasm."

—Winston Churchill

Wouldn't you love to wake up in the morning and go to work with people who have enthusiastic attitudes and positive energy? What about working somewhere that has a reputation for everyone wanting to work there because it is inspiring and fun? That would be great; but remember, that kind of enthusiasm has to start with you. Enthusiasm can breathe life into your work culture.

A few years ago, I was a speaker and vendor at the Missouri Student Counselors annual conference. One afternoon during a break, I met a counselor by the name of Tess, who just oozed with enthusiasm! She told me about a conference session she was teaching. This class had absolutely nothing to do with my career or life. But her enthusiasm for the subject made me decide to attend her session and even take notes. Enthusiasm is contagious! When you surround yourself with enthusiastic people, you feed off their energy.

When I was a kid, I don't know how many times I watched Walt Disney's animated movie *Jungle Book*. One of my favorite scenes (which I mimic to this day) involves vultures sitting on a tree branch. One of them yawns, hits the other vulture, and in a very low tone asks, "Hey, Flaps, what we gonna do?" To this the other replies, "I dunno, what do you wanna do?" and the conversation is repeated several times. The whole conversation reflects them being lifeless and bored. (It's also interesting that they eat dead things.) I don't want to live my life as lifeless and bored, eating the road kill of daily existence. I daily look for how that day can be an adventure, and I firmly believe you need to live each day with passion, enthusiasm, and expectation. Even on the job, you need to act alive, not like the living dead.

It's important to hang with people who don't act dead. Do you need to rise from the dead? Pull yourself out of the grave, get out of your comfort zone, and start living with enthusiasm. Contribute to a workplace culture where people love to come to work. Live in each moment and enjoy life with enthusiasm.

Is it easy to be enthusiastic, especially when your day is going downhill? Of course not. As I've said before, taking small actions can put you on a path to getting a better attitude. I like what Frank Bettger said in his book *How I Raised Myself from Failure to Success in Selling*: The number one rule of enthusiasm is "To be more enthusiastic, act more enthusiastic." When you're having "one of those days," think what small action you can do to spark enthusiasm. At the end of this chapter you'll find a list of ideas to take to help you out in the workplace.

Why do we need that enthusiasm? Enthusiasm will do the following for you:

* Give you energy

* Get you out of bed in the morning when you don't want to get up

* Combat fear

* Make you likeable

* Keep you motivated

* Help you not give up or quit

* Attract other enthusiastic people

According to *Life's Little Instruction Book*, "Be the most enthusiastic and positive person you know!" I think that would be a good sign to sit on your desk. Hobby Lobby would profit from making some of those signs.

> It's important to hang with people who don't act dead.

Remember the Chewbacca Mom? If you've never heard of her, then just Google "Chewbacca Mom." How did she set the record for getting the most viewed Facebook live videos of all time? It was her enthusiasm and laughter. The video became so popular that *Forbes* reported that the mask sold out from every online retailer. Candace Payne's life changed overnight because her enthusiasm for life was contagious. With both our last names being Payne, I wish I were related to her! I bet holiday meals are fun at her house.

Henry Ford said, "You can do anything if you have enthusiasm. Enthusiasm is the yeast that makes your hopes rise to the stars. With it, there is accomplishment. Without it there are only alibis."

There are many successful corporations that incorporate fun and enthusiasm into their workplace culture. I love the motto adopted by the Seattle Pike Place Fish Market in Seattle, Washington: "Work made fun gets done." Check out their You Tube videos. Cutting up fish all day wouldn't seem to be the type of place where you would think employees would have much fun—but they do.

"Make our customers happy—have a good time doing it," is the motto Cape Air follows to this day. The company hands out different types of fruit to passengers; then the passengers board the plane when their fruit is announced. "Would the bananas please board the aircraft?" Now wouldn't that get you excited about your upcoming trip? "Creativity and humor encourage enthusiasm, and enthusiasm is contagious," says founder and president Danielle Wolf.

One of the most stressful occupations is that of a police officer. I have several friends who are on the force, and of course it can be very dangerous. People with stressful jobs *especially* need fun, humor, and laughter. I absolutely love the viral video of the Norwalk Police Department lip sync to "Uptown Funk." They did it with one take, on a thirty-minute lunch break. You can tell they're having fun and there is so much energy. You smile and laugh as you watch the video. In an interview after they went viral, they said they wanted people to know that they were like anybody else that goes home after a day's work, and they too like to have fun.

Employees at eighty-one percent of Fortune's "100 Best Companies to Work For" say they work in a fun environment. In their book *Nuts*, Kevin and Jackie Freiberg wrote about the culture created by Herb Kelleher, founder of one of the most profitable companies, Southwest Airlines. Kelleher infused fun and enthusiasm in every department of the corporation. I love this quote from him: "What we are looking for, first and foremost, is a sense of humor. We hire attitudes."

In *Fun Is Good: How to Create Joy and Passion in Your Workplace*, author Mike Veeck talks about how infusing fun into the workplace can transform the entire company. Tom Peters, a noted writer on business management, says, "If you are working in a company that is not enthusiastic, energetic, creative, clever, curious and just plain fun, you've got troubles, serious troubles."

You might be sold on the idea of infusing fun and creativity into the workplace. But what are some simple ways to get started?

You must be intentional about finding the funny things in life. It's also the same in the workplace; you must be intentional about adding humor and laughter. Am I talking about pulling pranks and wasting time? No, of course not. There are appropriate and inappropriate ways to use humor as well as when to use it. You always need to be sensitive to people and the situation.

I believe humor and enthusiasm start at the top of the ladder in the workplace. In fact, if you are a leader, it must start with you. In Stephanie Schnurr's book *Leadership Discourse at Work: Interactions of Humour, Gender and Workplace*, she quotes Bob Ross, who said, "A leader without a sense of humor is like a lawn mower in a cemetery – they have lots of people under them, but nobody is paying them any attention." Humor helps leaders build rapport and trust with employees, promote open communication, and motivate employees. Leaders with a sense of humor will show employees that they are down to earth and just as human as they are.

A leader sets the tone in the organization. I've worked in companies where the CEO rarely leaves his office to go out among the employees. That's a huge mistake, as you cannot influence people or connect with them if you're never around them. Likewise, if you're not around them to show them your sense of humor, you stifle the amount of humor in your workplace. People won't see that you're really just like them (human, that is). You will develop loyal, productive, and engaged employees if on a consistent basis you incorporate humor and laughter into your work culture.

Humor and laughter in the workplace affects the bottom line. People are more productive when they're having fun, enjoying their jobs, and enjoying each other. People work better as a team when they work in a fun environment. When you laugh, oxygen flows to the brain, which will help you think better, feel better, and become very creative in problem-solving. Use creativity when adding humor to your workplace. Thirteenth-century surgeon Henri de Mondeville told jokes to his patients coming out of surgery because he felt laughter would aid their recovery.

Here are just a few ideas on what you can do. Try some, laugh, and you'll be glad you did:

1. Start a meeting with a funny You Tube video.

2. Create a humor bulletin board specifically for workplace humor.

3. Allow staff to personalize their work areas in fun ways.

4. Create funny computer screen savers.

5. Ask yourself...what's the one thing from this obstacle that I can take away, learn from, or laugh about?

6. Count to ten and imagine how funny it will seem a year from today.

7. Visualize an unfriendly co-worker as a cartoon character.

8. Make yourself laugh, even if you don't feel like it.

9. Share a funny story prior to a meeting starting.

10. Include fun activities in work plans—make fun a priority.

11. Create agendas with catchy titles, cartoons, jokes, or quotes.

12. Have a theme agenda using a movie title.

13. Include a humor break in every agenda.

14. Start or end meetings with a fun tradition.

15. Hold a "match the employee to the baby picture" contest.

16. Create campaign-style buttons for staff to wear to remind people to lighten up!

17. Create a fun company song, slogan, or cheer.

18. Create a giant wall mural where employees can add thoughts, ideas, quotes, or just color.

19. Devise some humorous contests for customers.

20. Auction off an ugly piggy bank or statue to be on someone's desk for a year, and donate the proceeds to a children's non-profit organization.

21. Make picture frames and have people make funny faces when their picture is taken.

22. Create a humorous newsletter or video to introduce change.

23. Create a quiz-style game show to help teach people about the changes going on.

24. Designate a "Fun Factor" person to promote humor.

25. Tape candy to memos, i.e. it's "Payday."

26. Reframe a negative event by looking at it through the eyes of your favorite comedian or superhero.

27. Create a humor bulletin board for clean good humor.

28. Form a singing group.

29. Have a fun awards ceremony midway through a particularly stressful period to energize everyone.

30. Brainstorm a humorous topic or play improv games before settling down to brainstorm the more serious topic at hand.

31. Use fun distractions like toys, wacky props, or costume items to encourage creative thinking during brainstorms.

32. Brainstorm the opposite of a problem to force a different perspective.

33. Form a Stress Busters Department.

34. Create your own "Top 10 Ways to Add Humor."

35. Have a "pick your nose" meeting, where everyone wears a clown nose, animal nose, etc.

36. End meetings with a dance.

37. Start a meeting out with Pictionary to introduce the agenda.

38. Hire a photographer to take pictures of employees in action and have a slide show at your next meeting or banquet.

39. Have an annual scavenger hunt.

40. Have a contest based on the American Institute top 100 funniest films.

41. Have a tailgate party.

42. Have a talent show.

43. Showcase everyone's kids.

44. Have a "guess the great-grandparent" picture contest.

45. Volunteer time and have fun.

46. Photoshop pictures of your team onto pictures of superheroes, celebrities, or historical figures.

47. Share a funny picture of the week from on-line.

48. Rent a costume photo booth for a day.

49. Hold a "grossest foods" dessert party.

50. Create a "Wanted" poster for a problem to be resolved.

51. Pass out play-dough to staff during a meeting.

52. Celebrate holidays, e.g., Star Wars day.

53. Include a funny picture in the middle of a boring slide presentation.

54. Do a flash-mob and post it on You Tube.

55. Before you get to work start singing Bob Marley's song, "Everything's gonna be all right!"

56. Free Food = Smiles.

57. Have a chili cook-off.

58. Preferred parking = happy employee.

59. Create a "Fun Team" or "Fun Committee" or "Fun Bunch."

60. Put fun or funny sticky notes on someone's computer.

61. Smile, Laugh, and Enjoy Your Day!

62. When you work with enthusiastic people, you can't help but be enthusiastic yourself.

CHAPTER 5

GRATITUDE WILL CHANGE AN ATTITUDE

Did you say thank you?

"Everyone has an invisible sign hanging around from their neck saying, 'Make me feel important.'"

—Mary Kay Ash, Founder of Mary Kay Cosmetics

A great way to boost employees' attitudes is by giving them a simple pat on the back, showing them appreciation and recognizing employees for what they do. In the grocery store one day, I saw an old friend and asked how her day was, as she looked a little frazzled. She said it was a normal super-busy day. However, she went on to talk about how she never saw the boss, the CEO of the company, and wished that someday her boss or someone in administration would just for once walk up to her and other staff and say, "Hey, you're doing a good job."

We all love to be celebrated and to be shown that we're appreciated. Recognizing employees on a consistent basis will not only boost morale but jump-start attitudes, boost productivity, benefit the bottom line, and lower employee turnover. Again, it doesn't take much time or money to recognize employees and co-workers for a job well done.

According to a 2016 survey from Globoforce Work Human Research Institute, employer recognition of employees significantly improves engagement, commitment, pride, and overall happiness. When you recognize employees or co-workers, and even customers or clients, you are highlighting their value. In the best-selling book *The Carrot Principle*, authors Adrian Gostick and Chester Elton write, "Great recognition can be done in a matter of moments—and it doesn't take budget-busting amounts of money." They also pointed out that employee recognition should be given on a consistent basis.

Recognizing people's accomplishments will fuel them to do more. You can say "Thanks for a job well done" by giving any of the following, but make sure you give the items with a thank you card or verbal thank you: You can give gift cards, fruit baskets, chocolate (dark chocolate: my favorite), and tickets to movie events. Be careful how many mugs and keychains you give out; you can only fill your cupboard with so much unmatched mugs and you only have so many keys. Or maybe have a masseuse come in and give chair massages. Or possibly greet employees at the door with coffee and Krispie Kreme donuts—not every day, of course, but often enough that the employees love showing up for work.

Recognizing employees on a consistent basis will not only boost morale but jump-start attitudes.

Our local hospital recently celebrated a big accomplishment with a photo booth which was rented. It was fun to see employees have fun, laugh, and get excited about what props they would wear to have their pictures taken.

Or maybe roll out a piece of red carpet for new employees on their first day of work, with welcome gifts on their desks or in their work area. Perhaps have a thank-you card saying, "Thanks for choosing us!" In my local Target store, you would see employees huddle and give high fives to each other. A friend of mine was thrilled recently to see his picture in the company's newsletter for a new product he designed. Again, we all love pats on the back.

At an awards banquet, show slides of employees through the year working hard (and throw in some funny pictures as well). Depending on the size of your company, you could provide profit-sharing. For a special event, rent a theatre and provide popcorn and drinks for everyone. All these are great ways to give an employee or co-worker a pat on the back. However, I believe the best demonstration of appreciation and recognition occurs when the boss, the leader, specifically the CEO of the company, goes to the work areas and verbally tells employees specifically what they're doing that makes a difference. That's what I call treating people like a diamond and making them feel valuable.

Recently I sat down with Randall Bradley, owner and manager of two Burger King franchises in both Iowa and Missouri. I was so impressed with his leadership skills, his ability to connect with his employees, the long retention of his employees, and his positive attitude towards his employees and customers. I asked him if he would write about his success and allow me to print it. This is what he had to say:

> When I won a "Franchisee of the Year, North America" award in my restaurant system, based on the Performance Index of my restaurants, other franchisees asked me how I won it. My answer was, "I realized years ago that I am not in the hamburger business, I am in the people business. Obviously, that is my customers, but it is also my managers, my team members and my vendors. If I do all of the people stuff right, I don't have to worry about hamburgers."
>
> I use Three Rights in my people management. I search until I find the Right People and give them all of the Right Training to do their job perfectly well; then I maintain the Right Relationship with them. This has

enabled me to have great operations while having average manager tenure of 20 years, with some team members
being with me 15 years. All of my managers started with
me as minimum wage team members. This has enabled
me to bring them up with my corporate culture and teach
them to do the same things with their people that I do (or,
at least, strive to do so).

My Manager Performance Appraisal has twelve categories. Two of them deal with Operations and Financial Goals, one addresses personal appearance, and one
deals with administrative accuracy. Eight of the twelve
deal with skills with people, because THAT is how we
succeed. Two of those on which I concentrate are "Image
with Crew" and "Positive Determination." These are the
two most responsible for my business success.

An example of Positive Determination: I saw a team
member make a sandwich extremely quickly, but some-
what messily. He was obviously working very hard to make
our Speed of Service goals. I could have ignored that and
just told him, "Hey, that last sandwich was messy; I need
you to improve your performance on eye appeal." Instead,
I said, "I noticed how fast you are at making sandwiches.
You are really helping us to make our speed of service
goals and I appreciate that. Now I want to add one more
thing: neatness and eye appeal. I am sure you agree we
would not want a customer to open a messy sandwich
and say, "Gee, I'm sure glad I got this mess quickly" (light
laughter is helpful here). So I need you to make sure your
sandwiches have great eye appeal. And when you add that
to your lightning quick speed, you are going to be one
AWESOME employee!"

So instead of feeling like he just got yelled at when
he was really trying to do well, he got a great compliment
along with some coaching and encouragement on how to

be even better. THAT is positive determination to meet your goals.

Isn't that a leader that sets the bar? Good people skills and maintaining a positive attitude bring many benefits to the workplace. Always remember: More than any other single factor, it is your attitude that makes the difference in your life and the lives of those around you.

Recognition, pats on the back, and expressions of thanks will make workplace zombies come back to life.

CHAPTER 6

POWER WORDS THAT GIVE LIFE

Did you say the magic words?

"Words are, of course, the most powerful drugs used
by mankind."

—Rudyard Kipling

Words are very powerful. A fascinating experiment was conducted years ago to measure people's capacity to endure pain.
Psychologists measured how long a barefooted person could
stand in ice water. They found one factor made it possible for
some people to stand in the ice water twice as long as others. Can you guess what that factor was? It was *encouraging
words*. Another psychologist, Henry H. Goddard, conducted
a study on energy levels in children, using an instrument he
called the "ergograph." Goddard discovered that when tired
children were given a word of praise or commendation, the
ergograph showed an immediate upward surge of energy in
the children. When the children were criticized or discouraged, the ergograph showed that their physical energy took a
nosedive. Isn't that still so true with us as adults? Our energy
goes way up when we get a positive word of encouragement.

Remember my Target and light switch stories in Chapter
Two? Words either ignite or extinguish your energy. Use your

words as a positive force to those around you. Remember that your words can bring healing. Your words can empower people to get through their day or even to do great things.

One negative phrase made by a co-worker either in person, in an email, or text can sour your whole day. Technology has transformed the way we communicate with other people. After stewing all night over a conversation with a friend, I got up early, slammed the keys on my keyboard with a response and before I knew it, I hit the send button. In looking back, I think I was like in slow motion putting my hands on my head and in that slow-motion sound and voice going, "N o o o o o o o o o." The friendship was difficult to repair after that and is still not the same.

In the workplace, it's very easy to let things just roll out of your mouth without thinking, or with your fingers, typing, for that matter. The result could be hurt feelings, anger, turmoil, and frustration. Before these things happen, here are four tips to help with communicating positively vs. negatively.

1. Pause and reflect before you hit the send button. Reread something you wrote and wait five minutes or even overnight before you send it. Would you want that email or text sent to you?

2. Remembering someone's name shows you value and respect them. Dale Carnegie said, "A person's name is to him or her the sweetest and most important sound in any language." Use people's names when possible. At work, instead of "Good morning," say, "Good morning, Joe." If you're going through a check-out lane and you see the cashier's name-tag, include the name in thanking him or her. Learn to remember a person's name, as it will make someone feel important, show respect, and make a connection with another person.

3. Think of phrases you can always have in your back pocket either when talking with someone who is constantly negative or if you yourself are tempted to be negative. Here are a few phrases you can use. Choose three to five and commit them to memory. The goal is to think before you speak and choose your words wisely.

I can certainly help you.
I appreciate you telling me this.
We can make it work.
Yes, absolutely!
Let's look at it from a different angle.
We learned from that experience.
You have good ideas.
Think of all the possibilities.
I completely agree with you.
That is an excellent suggestion.
Tell me one good win you had today.
Let's see how we can solve this issue together.
I can't speak to all that, but here's what I can tell you.
I need your help to clear up a potential misunderstanding.
Please and thank you.

4. Sometimes the best communication is to not say anything at all. William James said, "The art of being wise is the art of knowing what to overlook." Enough said.

**Pause and reflect before
you hit the send button.**

PART 3

WHAT IF YOU GET INFECTED BY THE LIVING DEAD?

CHAPTER 7

HELP! A ZOMBIE BIT ME!

Do you need CPR?

"The greatest discovery is that human beings can alter
their lives...simply by altering their attitude."

—Lee Iacocca

What happens if you get "bitten" by a Zombie? What if you
get infected with the zombie virus and begin to act like the
living dead? Perhaps at some point during your childhood or
adolescence, your mother pointed her finger at you and said,
"Get rid of that stinking attitude!" But the necessity of dealing with attitudes doesn't end with childhood. For the rest of
your life, you daily have to choose whether you're going to act
dead or alive. Perhaps I recognize zombie attitudes because
I struggled for years with acting like the living dead and
dealing with rotten, stinking attitudes. I wish I would have
known the information of this book early in life. I believe
we all get infected sometime or another with many of the
workplace zombies I mentioned in Chapter 2.

Let's say you're in a room with someone you care about.
Suddenly this person falls over and stops breathing. You
check his or her pulse but find none. You would immediately

call 911 and immediately start CPR. That person would be so appreciative that you brought him or her back to life.

However, there are other types of "pulses" we need to check. I challenge you to take your "attitude pulse" every single day. You do that by taking time to reflect on the zombie traits mentioned earlier. Are you acting like the ungrateful dead? (No, that's not a new rock band.) Are you seeing any of the negative traits that were listed earlier in this book taking over your attitude? Are you acting dead by dragging yourself through life with no spark, fun, or enthusiasm in you at all? If so, YOU NEED CPR! Not CPR for your heart, but CPR for your attitude.

What is CPR? Let's look at what each letter stands for.

CPR to Revive the Dead

C stands for CHOICE

Norman Vincent Peale said, "The only people without problems are those in a cemetery." Ultimately, no matter what circumstances or situation we are in, it's our own choice to act dead or alive. It's our choice to be negative or positive, to be or not to be a zombie. No one else is responsible for that choice but you. Others might influence you to make the choice, but you're it; you make the choice.

I mentioned earlier the friends who bought "my house." I think the number one reason why we become negative in our attitudes is because we are selfish and self-centered. We're thinking about #1 all the time (and we mistakenly think #1 is us). If we would get the focus off ourselves and make other people #1 by putting the focus on others, the zombies will die off. I love what John O'Leary says: "You can't always choose the path you walk in life. But you can always choose the manner in which you walk it."

There will be days when a co-worker, boss, customer, family member, friend, or neighbor will say something that rubs you the wrong way. It's easy to be influenced by other people; without realizing it, we let them determine our attitude. Sometimes, in some situations, you must choose simply to bite your lip. Choose the right path to walk down.

During the registration process for a doctor's appointment, I asked the young lady behind the counter how her day was going. She said she had a lady earlier who was very rude to her, and that encounter put her in a sour mood. However, she also said that she decided she was not going to allow that lady to ruin her day, so she chose to get into a good mood. I said, "Good for you!" Her attitude ended up helping both of us—it helped her by getting her back into a good mood for the day, and it helped me by giving me an example of how one's choices can turn one's day around.

A few years ago, a spider bit me under one eye and left two pretty good-sized craters—at least, they looked like craters to me. I went to a specialist and, while there, thought to myself, "This doctor is one of the most chipper and happy doctors I've ever met." I asked Dr. Koch if he ever got a bad attitude at work. He said, "Of course! But I never let anyone see it." He makes the choice every day to remain alive, not to act like the living dead. (By the way, Dr. Koch helped the craters disappear.)

You are the one who chooses and decides every single day of your life what kind of mood you are going to be in, regardless of **It's our own choice to act dead or alive.** any situation. Abraham Lincoln said, "Most folks are about as happy as they make up their minds to be." You make the choice for your attitude.

A friend of mine, John Holmes, is an American Airlines pilot. He tells me that airplanes have "an attitude." The "attitude indicator" on the control panel of an aircraft is the most vital instrument for a pilot. The attitude indicator is circular with the top half blue, which represents the sky, and the bottom half is brown, which represents the ground. There is a line in the middle, which is the artificial horizon, representing the real horizon.

The "attitude" is based on the roll and pitch of the aircraft. For the roll, if the nose of the aircraft goes up or down, it is indicated on the indicator and considered either a nose-high or nose-down attitude. The wings going up or down is known as the pitch. This instrument is especially helpful if it is raining, snowing, foggy, or cloudy, as the attitude indicator will let the pilot know the position of the aircraft even when the position cannot be seen with the eyes. During flight, a large aircraft makes hundreds of automatic adjustments based on the attitude indicator.

The bottom line is this: The performance of the aircraft is determined by its attitude. Isn't that so interesting! I believe it's the same in the workplace. Our performance is based on our attitude!

Well, I decided I needed to see the inside of an airplane's cockpit to check it out. I called our local airport to see if I could borrow an airplane (it is a very small airport). Before I knew it, I was up in the air with a pilot getting my first flying lesson! I discovered firsthand that the attitude indicator is definitely important if you want the aircraft to fly correctly.

It's the same in life; we need to pay attention to the attitude indicator on the inside of each one of us. If we pay attention to it and make the necessary adjustments (or choices), we will go high in life and be successful.

CPR

P stands for PERSPECTIVE

According to Webster's, the word "perspective" means "the capacity to view things in their true relations or relative importance." The Oxford Dictionary of the English Language defines perspective as "a particular attitude toward or way of regarding something." What is your perspective on your life, your circumstances, the people around you, or maybe the rude comment one of your co-workers made about you?

Ironically, the first day I began writing this section is the day that I first heard of and listened to John O'Leary. What an inspiration! At age nine, he was severely burned with third-degree burns over 87% of his body; he had less than 1% chance to live. He couldn't talk, move, eat, drink, or see for five months; all his fingers were blown off during an explosion while playing with fire. He miraculously lived to tell his inspiring story of overcoming the odds. (Make sure you read his book, *On Fire*.)

After hearing him speak I gave myself a talk. "Wake-up call, Desirae Lynn Payne!" (Remember when your mother would say your whole name when you were a kid—you knew you were in trouble.) "I'm talking to you, Desirae! You have so much to be thankful for. You have fingers to type this, you don't have burn scars, and above all, you never had your child struggle for life on a burn unit. Life is good; you are so blessed!" It's very easy to lose perspective of your blessed life and begin to develop the wrong attitude or wrong viewpoint of it.

As a magician for over twenty years, I love doing illusions. I like to trick people's brains into seeing something that is not there. Sometimes our brains trick us into thinking we don't have enough in life. Sometimes we're tricked into thinking our life is miserable. But all of us need to wake ourselves up sometimes. Get a new perspective on life today! The stupid little comment your co-worker said is just that, stupid and little. Don't blow things out of proportion and be tricked into thinking petty things that happen at work are big things. I saw a sign one time that said, "Will this really matter in one year?" That's a good question to ask yourself quite frequently.

Probably the most inspiring person I've ever heard speak is Nick Vujicic, a man born without legs or arms. When you watch Nick on YouTube surfing, sky-diving, swimming, playing soccer, and living life with an overcoming attitude, you are inspired. There is never a reason for me to have a bad attitude after hearing Nick speak.

When you have a bad day at work, I encourage you to put the day in perspective. My sister has been a 911 dispatcher in Orlando, Florida, for over ten years. She gets over 200 calls a day. Sometimes I ask her, "So what's the crime like in Orlando this week?" When I used to ask this question, she would usually report teens running away or cars broken into. Today, however, she reports a shooting every week. Her co-workers took the calls from victims at the Pulse Bar a few years ago where 49 people were tragically murdered. On the phone the dispatchers could hear gun shots, screams, and even people's interactions with the killer.

Are you really having a bad day when the copier doesn't work, you're running late for a meeting, your boss asks one more thing from you, or a co-worker says something unkind to you? I don't think you would trade jobs with my sister on June 12, 2016, in Orlando, Florida.

I believe you can shift your perspective from negative to positive. When I see my eye doctor, he has me look at the reading chart through many different lenses until something becomes crisp and clear. If you struggle with a negative attitude, try different "lenses," looking at situations until you get a better perspective. Remember that taking action steps gets your emotions and feelings moving the right direction. Bring life back to your attitude by changing your perspective.

CPR

R stands for. . .

Before I tell you what R stands for, let me ask the *Walking Dead* fans a question. How do you kill a zombie? That's right; you have to shoot or stab them in the brain. I know, totally disgusting...Ugh. But let me make the point: All attitudes start in your brain. They begin with how you think. Mahatma Gandhi said, "A man is but a product of his thoughts. What he thinks, he becomes." Earl Nightingale said, "You become what you think" and Solomon said, "As a man thinks in his heart, so is he." Your actions are the result of the way you think. American psychologist and philosopher William James once said, "The greatest discovery of my generation is that a human being can alter his life by altering his attitude."

During the writing of this book, my husband and I were changing what we ate as a sort of detox program to clean up our digestive systems and clear out any toxins in our body. The detox involved deleting dairy, breads, certain grains, processed foods, desserts, and all fruits except berries, green apples, and green bananas, due to their low sugar content. I can't say it was an easy eight weeks, but it paid off. Fewer toxins meant more energy and feeling better.

Many times, our minds become toxic with negativity. It's very important to detox and clear any toxic thinking out of our minds. With that said, I now bring you the letter R in CPR, which stands for **REBOOT YOUR BRAIN**.

CHAPTER 8

REBOOT THE BRAIN

Do you know how to kill a zombie?

"Life is 10% what happens to you and
90% how you react to it."

—Charles Swindoll

How would you reboot your brain? First, let's look at how we reboot our computers. When your computer acts wonky, freezes up, or acts lifeless, you must reboot it. To do that you have to hit CTRL, ALT, DEL (Control, Alternate, and Delete) keys. When that happens, the computer shuts down, deletes the present information, and starts over again. That's what we need to do with the negative attitudes in our brain. We need to CONTROL what we're thinking about, ALTERNATE negative thoughts with positive thoughts, and DELETE the negative attitude. Is that simple? Not always. During the toxin cleanse Craig and I did, there were many times when I really wanted chocolate, sundaes, Ben & Jerry's ice cream, BBQ ribs dripping with sauce, and homemade baked bread. But self-control is the key to accomplishing the goal of feeling better and reaching better health.

It takes huge amounts of self-control to not think negatively when people treat us unfairly, disrespectfully, or in a mean way. In the past I allowed thoughts of those situations to swirl non-stop in my brain. I've gone to bed thinking about hurtful situations and during the day remained obsessed with them. These constant battles in our minds trigger different emotions and attitudes such as the ones listed in Chapter 1. It's easy to have a conversation with that person in your mind, visualizing what you would say if you could say what you wanted to say right to his or her face. You rehearse it and nurse it and it grows bigger and bigger until your actions mimic what you think. The unforgiveness, bitterness, and angry feelings can lead to high blood pressure, upset stomach, insomnia, and more, which we'll discuss further in a later chapter. We need to remember: If we change our minds and change our attitudes, we will change our lives.

When the brain is filled with toxic negativity, it zaps energy; then there is little energy to focus on problem-solving, productive thoughts, positive emotions, or others. Get your brain rebooted and destroy the zombie brain attitudes.

Here are three guaranteed ways to reboot your brain: Be grateful, change your mindset to value others, and laugh more.

Reboot Your Brain #1: Be Grateful

After I started my humor therapy program as a professional clown, I met an oncologist who would meet with me every morning and give me a list of patients she wanted me to visit. One day she told me about a woman she wanted me to see. I started to go to the room when the doctor stopped me and said, "Wait, I need to talk with this patient first. I'm going to tell her she's going to die. Are you okay with going in and talking with her afterwards?"

Well, what would be your reaction to that request? In my mind I thought, "Why on earth do you want me to go in now?" But I smiled as best as I could and said, "No problem." When she went in, I leaned against the wall wondering what on earth I would say. It just didn't seem like the right time for me to go in as a clown. When the doctor came out, she nodded at me. I waited a little bit before I went in, praying for the right words.

I knocked on the door and peeked in. I saw an older woman, perhaps in her late eighties, sitting up in bed with her legs drawn up to her. Her son, probably in his sixties, was standing over her. Both had tears in their eyes. Immediately, however, the patient perked up, smiled, and said, "Hi, do I know you?" I slowly entered the room and smiled back and said, "No, I don't think we've ever met." I introduced myself and we had some small chit-chat.

Normally I don't sit on a patient's bed, but I sat on the edge of the bed, looked at her, and said, "I understand you just got some very bad news." All of a sudden she burst out in tears and through her sobs kept saying, "You don't understand. You don't understand." Then she said something that surprised me. "You don't understand. I've spent so much money on the shopping network!"

I just sat and looked at her, a little puzzled, thinking, "That's probably the last thing I'd be thinking about right now." I looked over at her son, who had his mouth hanging open and looking at his mother as though she weren't all there. Then all of a sudden, he got this huge smile from ear to ear and gave me the look that said: This was indeed classic for his mother to say. I smiled back. Taking her hand into mine, I looked her in the eye and said, "You know what? That's okay!" She broke into a huge grin and we continued to talk for a few more minutes. She then had me say the 23rd Psalm with her before I left.

On my way home, I was grateful that I had provided smiles for those two during a difficult situation, but even more grateful that I had walked out that day with no doctor telling me, "You're going to die." After working with patients for so many years, I always left each day with a fresh perspective of gratitude. I am grateful that I didn't have a family member in the hospital, that I wasn't just diagnosed with cancer, that I had all my limbs, or that I did not have a disease. Several years ago, I started a "gratitude journal" and I strive daily to write down what I'm thankful to God for. It's amazing when you go back a few years and read what you wrote; you are reminded how blessed your life is. You then become even more grateful.

There have been numerous times over the years that I've given "gratitude journals" to individuals who acted like the living dead; however, I've then discovered that to this day they've never written one thing down that they're thankful for.

> **If we change our minds and change our attitudes, we will change our lives.**

Many times in life you have to make yourself do things even when you don't feel like doing them—such as writing down what you are grateful for even when you don't feel all that grateful. Taking action steps will help change your emotions, mind, and attitude.

I mentioned earlier Dr. Koch, who said he doesn't let it show if he has a bad attitude; this doctor also said one of the best ways to keep his attitude up with his co-workers or patients is to say "Thank you" quite often. He said you must constantly show your appreciation to people. In turn, people's attitudes will be positive. I had a job once in which the boss never said thank you for anything. She told someone one day that you don't tell someone thank you for a job they're required to do. However, the oil of thankfulness really does lubricate the workplace, reducing friction. Always remember to say thank you and show gratitude.

Remember my videographer, the fellow who is in the top ten most enthusiastic people I know? He told me about a friend of his whose eight-year-old daughter was going through a powerful course of chemotherapy. They were thrilled when they switched her over to a regular chemotherapy regimen. After having that conversation, he thought, "Everything is good in my life." This is said by someone who as a child lost his mother to cancer. Isaac's positive attitude and enthusiasm is so contagious!

"Gratitude will change your attitude," says Nick Vujicic. Nick's company is called "Attitude is Altitude." You will reboot your mind when you are grateful and show gratefulness to others in the workplace.

Reboot Your Brain #2: Have a MINDSET to ADD VALUE to People

When I worked for Royal Caribbean Cruise Lines, I was part of the Enrichment Staff, which allowed me to be a regular guest when I wasn't entertaining families. One day I went up to the guest services counter to ask a simple question. When I approached the counter, the gentlemen behind it gave me an amazing smile. In his French accent he asked me, "Madam, how is your day today?" I replied that I was having an awesome day, to which he responded, "But how can I make it even better than that?" It took me by surprise. Immediately, I knew that this guy was going to take good care of me! This guy was treating me like the most important person on the cruise at that moment. He made me feel **valued.**

When my family and I were in England a few years ago, we took a one-day tour across the English Channel to visit Paris. I loved every minute of the trip, especially when we got bumped up to first-class! After having lunch on the Eiffel Tower, the last thing the tour guide told us was that we could either go shopping or go to the Louvre. It was a no-brainer for my husband and son, as they were going to the most famous museum in the world. But my daughter and I were torn. When would we ever be in Paris to go shopping again? (Let me emphasize that again: SHOPPING IN PARIS!

Ooh la la!) On the flip side, when would we ever get the opportunity to see the famous smile of DaVinci's *Mona Lisa*? After we went back and forth with the options, I told Erin rather frankly, "We're going to do both!" We ran down to the shops, made sure we bought at least two or three things, and then went to the Louvre. We briskly walked and even jogged to get to Mona, and thankfully, we weren't stopped by the French police. The painting is not by the front door, so we were huffing and puffing when we finally got to the room. When we got there, it was packed with people, so we were on our tiptoes to see the famous lady.

The history behind this famous Leonardo da Vinci painting is fascinating. The picture was actually stolen in 1911. Two years went by before the true culprit was discovered, an Italian petty criminal called Vincenzo Perugia, who had moved to Paris in 1908 and worked at the Louvre for a time. He went to the gallery in the white smock that all the employees there wore and hid until it closed for the night, when he removed the *Mona Lisa* from its frame. When the gallery reopened, he walked unobtrusively out with the painting under his smock, attracting no attention, and took it to his lodgings in Paris.

When you go into the Louvre now, it's interesting to see the painting under high security. Mona is behind bullet-proof glass. In front of her is a wooden railing, she is roped off, there are security cameras, and the room is filled with security guards. Mona is not leaving the building! Today the *Mona Lisa* is valued at close to one billion dollars and has the highest insurance value for any painting in history.

That's pretty mind-boggling, that a painting would carry that much value. Since the day she was stolen and found, people put more value on her. People put value on so many THINGS in life. But after that day I begin to think about how important it is to put high value on people. Just like people added value to Mona, we too should add value to people by the way we look at them, treat them, and talk to them.

Workplace zombies **subtract** value from people. Start getting a mindset that everyone you work with is very valuable! Okay, maybe you don't like the people in the cubicles next to you, but if you look at them with value, you will treat them differently. How would you want to be treated? It is interesting that the "Golden Rule" is recited in one form or another in almost every religion around the world. Treat people with value, the way you yourself would want to be treated with value by them.

Consider Dr. Mukkada, an anesthesiologist I work with every week. After talking with the patients, he always ends by shaking their hands and saying, "We're going to take good care of you." By this very simple action, he's showing the patient, "I value you and want you to know that I'm going to take good care of you." Every day when you're at work, think about your customers, clients, students, patients, co-workers, or whomever you work with, and ask yourself a simple question: How can I add value to someone today? You add value to people by letting them know how valuable they are. Every time you do that, you're getting the focus off of you and onto someone else's value.

Sometimes it's just small gestures that let people know if they are valued or not. As for small gestures, Dr. Ortell, one of the busiest surgeons at our local hospital, always takes the time to say hello, talks with the nurses and me, and even tries to tell us jokes. (Let's just say he's an amazing surgeon and telling jokes is not his gift.) After my recent endoscopy, he, like Dr. Mukkada, said at least twice, "We're going to take very good care of you." It doesn't take a lot of effort to show people they are valued.

Recognizing people on their birthdays not only shows you value them, but can be fun. At our local Hy-Vee grocery store, you will hear someone say "Happy Birthday" to a fellow employee over the intercom. Gathering around a birthday employee and singing the song only takes fifteen seconds. That doesn't take much time to put a smile on someone's face, turn his face red, and put a spotlight on his value.

But how do you value people who clash with your personality or rub you the wrong way on a consistent basis? It starts with changing your mindset and looking at them as though they are a diamond. Once I saw the largest diamond in the world, in London, England. In fact, the Queen happens to own that big rock; it's called "The Cullinan Diamond," valued today at four hundred million dollars. It is heavily guarded and behind glass. When people shuffle by to gaze upon it, you can hear the oohs and awes, and sense the attitude of respect for this priceless jewel.

But isn't it more important to value people even above diamonds? If you go through life treating people like priceless diamonds, your life will be different.

Even with the physician I mentioned earlier who always abruptly cut me off, I always tried to make eye contact and say, "Good morning" even if I only got a slight nod back in return. I tried to value him with my time, even if it was only for a few seconds. Look for the good in everyone. Even Luke Skywalker told his father, Darth Vader, "I know there is good in you, Father." Even when your "Darth Vader" co-workers walk in the door, swirling their capes and breathing heavily, find some good in them.

Every time I've bought a new car, I thought I was the only one in town with that model and color. To my surprise, when I drove off the lot, I saw cars everywhere with the same model and color that I had never seen before. You can blame this on your RAS. The Reticular Activating System is a bundle of nerves at our brainstem that filters out unnecessary information, so the important stuff gets through. The RAS takes what you focus on and creates a filter for it. Then it sifts through information and presents to you only what is important. That's why after you buy that car you become aware of all the other cars that look just like yours. I believe we can use the RAS to look for the good in people. You must filter out the bad and be *intentional* to become aware of the good in those people who act like the living dead.

In the book *How to Be Like Walt*, author Pat Williams writes about the life of Walt Disney and gives many examples of how Walt took the time to value people. Walt made it a point to call each employee by name. When Disneyland grew in size and employees, it was known that Walt would go into Human Resources at night and memorize the names of employees with their pictures. He knew that calling someone by name shows you value them, and wanted to be an example of this.

One of my favorite actors is Bill Murray, especially in his great film *Groundhog Day*. His character, Phil Connors, is an arrogant and selfish TV weatherman who, during an assignment covering the annual Groundhog Day event, is caught in a time loop, repeating the same day over and over again. His arrogance and selfish attitude contribute to him living his nightmare again and again. Like Phil Connors, sometimes we are oblivious to how we act and come across to people with our negative attitudes. It's easy to live in our bubble of "Me, myself, and nobody else." After reliving his miserable day countless times, he finally comes to the realization that a fulfilled life is about others. When you forget yourself and put other people first and value other people, your whole life will change for the better. Your attitude will transform from negative to positive. As the movie concludes, you see Phil appreciating everything that life has to offer.

I encourage you today to reflect on your own attitude. Remember to daily take your "attitude pulse" and begin to intentionally value other people, get the focus off yourself, and enjoy your life.

Reboot Your Brain #3: Laugh Often

The best way to reboot your brain is with laughter. Laughter can change your brain chemistry and your attitude very quickly. When I was the patient advocate working at a hospital, there was a professional clown on staff by the name of Dr. Bugg. He was absolutely amazing with his gift to bring laughter to patients, families, and staff. Since I dealt with patient complaints, there were days I would track him down to go in to talk with a patient who was unhappy. He would do his magic and completely change the atmosphere of the room. You would hear giggles and laughter up and down the hallways.

One night I was asked to do the entertainment at a banquet that Dr. Bugg was attending, which was a bit intimidating. However, I had done mime for many years, so I did a few mime skits. Afterwards, Dr. Bugg made a bee-line up to me and wanted to know who taught me what I had just done. I told him I had just figured it out on my own years earlier, with no actual training. He then asked me an unusual question: "Have you ever thought about going to clown college?" I thought, now that is the dumbest thing I've ever heard of; besides, my husband doesn't like clowns. [Or mimes—husband's editorial comment.]

Dr. Bugg continued to "bug" me about it for weeks afterwards. To make a long story short, I ended up going to clown college to become a professional clown. That one question he asked me changed my life.

Dr. Bugg then mentored me to take his place at the hospital. Throughout, this experience has been one of the most amazing and satisfying journeys of my life. My professional name became "Dizzy," primarily due to the fact that my mother-in-law never could get "Desi" right and called me "Dizzy" instead. Dizzy became my character, and I weekly infused laughter into the lives of patients, family members, and staff. With that said, providing humor and laughter for twenty years taught me that without a shadow of doubt, laughter is powerful. While visiting patients, I saw before my eyes anxiety dissipate, stress reduced, children stop crying, and patients and families relax when they laughed. For the record, I wasn't one of those scary creepy clowns or the stereotyped alcoholic bum clown. And I've never seen the older or newer version of the movie, *IT*. From what I understand, I would not recommend it unless you want to be terrified of clowns for the rest of your life.

From a physiological standpoint, when you laugh many regions of your brain are involved, and the neurotransmitters, endorphins and dopamine are released and make you feel better. In fact, laughter brings so many benefits for a person emotionally and physically. Laughter even benefits you in the workplace. Here are some laughter benefits—it is a:

Key component to a happy life
Morale booster
Natural pain-killer
Mini-vacation from problems
Memory booster

What does laughter do for you? Laughter:

Boosts profitability
Boosts T-cells
Breaks down barriers
Burns calories
Contributes to a positive attitude
Creates a connection with people
Creates an inspiring and energized place to work
Decreases anxiety
Dilates blood vessels
Enhances communication

Facilitates open communication
Gives us more energy
Gives us a light-hearted workout
Gives us a natural high
Helps us connect with others
Helps us manage change
Helps us live longer
Improves cardiac health
Improves innovation
Increases oxygen intake
Increases employee engagement
Inspires creativity
Is contagious
Lowers blood pressure
Makes us look younger
Makes us more approachable
Makes us more productive
Makes us more resilient
Massages our internal organs
Kills pain naturally
Produces a general sense of well-being
Promotes teamwork
Reduces depression
Reduces stress hormones
Rejuvenates, restores, and relaxes the brain
Sends oxygen to our brains
Is the best medicine
Triggers the release of endorphins and dopamine
Unplugs the brain from difficult tasks
Uplifts other people's spirits
Works your abs

So how can we laugh more? Well, it starts with some humor.

Do you have a sense of humor? You might know people who definitely do not. "A sense of humor," according to C.W. Metcalf and Roma Felible in their book *Lighten Up*, is a "set of survival skills that keeps us fluid and flexible instead of allowing us to become rigid and breakable." After speaking at a leadership retreat, a woman came up to me and confided that she struggled with being humorous and wanted to know how to be funny. First, not everyone is born a witty and funny comedian like Robin Williams, Jerry Seinfeld, George Carlin, Eddie Murphy, Joan Rivers, Steve Martin, or Jim Carrey. So, what about the rest of us?

You first need to know what humor is. Humor is a comic, absurd, or incongruent quality that causes amusement. I know people with a great sense of humor and some with absolutely no sense of humor at all. Humor can be found by looking through a "Humor Lens" to find the funny. That's what a comedian does. They take any situation in life and find the funny. You can, too. Humorous things are out there; you just have to look for them. Even Dr. Seuss says, "From there to here, from here to there, funny things are everywhere."

The average four-year-old laughs 300 times a day. The average 40-year-old? Only four. One of the reasons for this is that a child lives in the moment. We're so busy, the stressors of life and our workload prevent us from living in the moment. When you live in the moment, you can see funny things quicker than not.

A few years ago, I was driving to a speaking engagement in Northern Iowa on a back road surrounded by corn stalks. I drove by a house and had to turn around to go back and take a picture. The run-down house, which had old cars parked in the front yard, a very old barn, and tons of stuff piled everywhere, had a huge sign blocking the driveway that had these words spray-painted: "STAY OUT, NO TRESPASSING, GET LOST!" Do you think he's made his point? I shared that with several people because I thought it was funny. Sharing funny things is a great way to share humor and laughter.

Sometimes when you're going through a tough situation, you think, "Someday I will laugh at this." Remember when I told you I heard John O' Leary speak for the first time? After his phenomenal keynote speech, to everyone's surprise he went over and played the piano with hands that had fingers blasted off from the explosion that crippled him. He played his mother's favorite song, "Amazing Grace." As he began to play, tears were streaming down people's faces; you could have heard a pin drop had he not been playing the piano. Halfway through the song, someone started to cough. It started to become irritating; then the coughing spell went on and on and got louder and louder during this very inspirational moment. Everyone looked back at the cougher and gave her "the look." Finally, she made her way out the back door.

You guessed it. Yes, it was me hacking all the way out. I couldn't believe that of all times, I had taken a drink of water and it went down the wrong pipe. I can laugh today about it (but not then).

Remember, you don't have to be stand-up comic to be humorous. Share funny stories, do funny things, share a funny You Tube video, do something that puts a smile on someone's face. I remember when I was fixing salmon for dinner one night, my husband walked in and picked up the slab of salmon and tapped me on the shoulder with it. Thinking that was a strange thing to do, I asked him what he was doing. He said that was a "Salmon Patty." You might not think that's funny, but it did make me laugh. Unexpected things can be funny!

A few years ago, I was watching one of the morning news shows and Jay Leno was a guest. It was one of those teary, feel-good stories where he has just given one of his cars to a veteran. He said something which caught my attention. He said, "If a day has gone by and I haven't been able to help someone smile or laugh, I haven't done my job." I thought, WOW! What a great philosophy to adapt into our lives—making it a goal that the attention gets off yourself, and making a goal each day to make sure you help at least one person smile or laugh.

I'll end this chapter with a story which I hope will make you smile or laugh. For years I've done motivational programs in schools with all-school assemblies. About fifteen years ago, I was in an elementary school doing a magic show with a super-hero theme. The show was called "Super Heroes are Super Respectful." The grand finale was to bring up four elementary students and dress them up like super heroes. I would then walk between each child and have them pull out a large silk cloth with a letter imprinted on it. Magically, they spell the word HERO. I look at the audience in pride and say, "Kids, don't forget! When you are super respectful you are a super ...." and they finish the line. When I did this, nobody responded. Thinking it was odd, I said it again louder, "Kids, don't forget! When you are super respectful you are a super........" and again, nothing—until I saw some teachers putting their hands over their mouths and giggling, and little first graders on the front row starting to pronounce the word as loudly as they could as new readers. The letters did not come out as planned. Instead of HERO, they spelled out H O R E. Well, even though there is no W on the front, the little children were yelling WHORE! WHORE! WHORE! After I discovered this, I'm sure I turned very faint and starting switching letters around as fast as I could, chanting as loudly as I could, HERO, HERO, HERO! In my mind I was also envisioning these sweet little children going home and telling their parents that when they are respectful they will be super whores. It was truly a day I won't forget, and still laugh about today.

Remember to do these three things to roboot your brain and destroy a zombie attitude:

1. Be grateful,

2. Change your mindset to value others, and

3. Laugh more.

PART 4

WILL YOU CHOOSE
TO BE
DEAD OR ALIVE?

CHAPTER 9

GET RID OF STRESS

Does stress affect your attitude?

"Take control of your stress before it takes control of you."
—Paul Huljich

A friend of mine baked a cake that weighed half a ton—literally. She was honored to be invited to bake and decorate the cake for the President's Inaugural Ball in Washington, D.C., in 1989. Without including the work on the blueprints, it was a labor-intensive thirteen full days around the clock to make the cake. Every part of it was edible, including the President's Seal and even the tiny pages of the Bible written in licorice-flavored ink. Today, there is a replica of that cake in the National Smithsonian Museum.

It was a very high-security operation, with Secret Service men (with dogs) watching her every move. The last thing she needed to do was to attach the word "President" in front of "George W. Bush" on the front of the cake. Also, at that time, one of the Secret Service men told her that the President was coming and going to walk through the door any moment and that she needed to hurry up. She noticed she was out of icing in the bag, which she needed to attach the letters. She turned to her assistant and asked her if she would load a pastry bag with an icing tip #22. Without even thinking, her assistant yelled back, "Donna, I have a loaded 22 to finish off the President!"

Within moments, she was surrounded by Secret Service men with their guns out. My five-foot-tall, petite little friend jumped up to one of them, grabbed him by the arm, and said, "I'm not trying to shoot the President!" Of course, when the FBI agents heard that, they released the dogs! During the chaos, they finally understood what the assistant meant and re-holstered their guns. I asked her, "Did they console you, hug you, or say I'm sorry?" She told me no, they were pretty serious, and went back to their posts.

Well, she did indeed, finish off the President. President Bush came through and absolutely loved the cake. She met up with her husband at the ball, still a little shook up, and told him the frightening story. A little bit later, one of the Secret Service men walked up to her, put his hand on her shoulder, and asked if she was okay. He then told her that he almost shot her. Talk about stress on the job! There was a happy ending; my friend and the Secret Service man ended up becoming life-long friends, with him even attending her daughter's wedding. As she was leaving the ball, a reporter stopped her and asked her how she felt about making the First Cake, and if she'd do it again. She replied, "That's the last and I'm bushed!"

I can't even begin to imagine the stress that Donna experienced when all those guns were pointing at her and she saw her life pass before her eyes. On the other hand, sometimes our stress level is determined just by an accumulation of the little things in life that grate on us and get on our nerves on a daily basis.

I'm always intrigued to find out what stresses people out and what they do about it. One day I asked a guy in his early thirties what stressed him out. Without hesitation in a rather sharp tone he said, "My wife, my kid, and my job!" I asked him what he did about it and he said, "Nothing! That's why I'm so angry all the time!" Wow, if that dude doesn't learn how to minimize, eliminate, and manage stress, it's going to be detrimental to his health, his job, and his family.

According to the Oxford Dictionary, stress is "a state of mental or emotional strain or tension resulting from adverse or very demanding circumstances." From my own experience, stress is probably the number one killer of my attitude. I emerge from the dead as a zombie with little tolerance, a short fuse, and no patience at all. Over the years, stress has affected my health in many ways, so I've made it a priority to learn to minimize, eliminate, and manage the stress in my life.

When your brain perceives any type of stressor, it quickly begins to respond by sending an alarm through your nervous system to alert your body to react. Your breathing rate increases, blood pressure goes up, blood flows to your muscles, blood sugar levels increase, muscles tense up, adrenal glands release stress hormones, hands and feet begin to sweat, and your heart rate increases. Why is that? Because your body is preparing to either run or respond due to the fight or flight response.

This was a good thing when we were in London, England, several years ago. We were underground getting ready to climb into "The Tube," which is the underground rail system. (Of course, we saw a rat run across the platform, which made it more authentic.) When the doors opened up, my son got on and took a seat, as well as myself. My husband took a step up, dragging behind our enormous suitcases, when the door quickly shut on those suitcases. Immediately, I jumped up as well as those sitting around me, and we started prying the doors open. All the fight or flight physical responses were responding as needed because the real problem was that my 13-year-old daughter was still standing on the platform with a look of terror on her face. In a split second my husband leaned over the luggage, grabbed my daughter by the shirt, and hoisted her over the luggage. The luggage was pulled in, the doors closed, and we sped off. For a while, my husband and I sat in shock, envisioning our daughter getting smaller and smaller as we pulled away and what could have happened had we left her in London, England. What's interesting though, is that about fifteen minutes after that stressful incident, all of our fight or flight responses settled down, our blood pressure and heartbeat were back to normal, and we were laughing about it.

Our bodies are fearfully and wonderfully created to deal with stressful situations. What our bodies were NOT created for is to live in a fight or flight response on a daily basis. This type of stress over time causes wear and tear externally and internally. This non-stop stress will have your stress hormones pumping non-stop as well. If that happens, those high levels of stress hormones can result in your health being compromised. If you don't learn to minimize, eliminate, or manage stress in your life, you could develop any of the following chronic problems (and this is only a partial list!):

Adrenal fatigue
Allergies
Anxiety
Autoimmune diseases
Cancer
Chronic fatigue
Decreased libido
Depression
Diabetes
Dizziness
Fibromyalgia
Gastrointestinal disorders
Headaches
Heart attack

Hostility
Hypertension
Immune system lowered
Irritability
Memory impairment
Muscle tension
Pain
Panic disorders
Skin conditions
Sleep disorders
Stroke
Weight gain

Physician and New York Times best-selling author Daniel Amen addresses chronic stress in his book, *Change Your Brain, Change Your Body*. He writes that chronic stress harms the brain: "Chronic stress constricts blood flow to the brain, which lowers overall brain function and prematurely ages the brain." This is due to the effects of excessive amounts of the stress hormone cortisol, which has negative consequences for both cognitive function and emotional balance.

Several years ago I began forgetting why I walked into another room. I became concerned that I left the stove or iron on when I left home or forgot whom I was calling when I was put on hold for an extensive period of time. After a visit to my doctor, I waited until the very end to express my concerns. This doctor, whom I've had for many years, started laughing. I must have looked surprised when he laughed because he said, "I've been talking with you for the last twenty minutes and nothing concerns me at all that you have Alzheimer's disease." He then told me about backing out of the drive-way in the middle of the night at a high speed to get to the hospital for an emergency, forgetting his son's brand-new parked car in the drive-way, and smashing into it. He told me that stress causes memory issues and that he suspected my lifestyle and fast pace were affecting my memory. I left with peace of mind.

Ironically, what are the odds that I'm going through my edits of my first manuscript of this book and can't find Chapter 9? After spending an hour tearing up my office trying to find the hardcopy with all my changes, I decided to go through the trash and sure enough, there it was. I had decided to pitch it and start over. At the same time, my computer wasn't cooperating, kept freezing up, the autosave wasn't working, and I kept losing what I typed every thirty minutes. I finally rebooted the crazy thing and restarted it. (Hmmmmmmm.....I think I talked about the importance of rebooting in a previous chapter.)

Further, several years ago, the same time I was concerned about Alzheimer's, I was having numerous health issues, difficulty getting up in the morning after sleeping all night, and countless sinus issues. After seeing several specialists, one of them did some extensive testing and concluded that I had adrenal fatigue. The adrenal glands sit over the kidneys, where they play a significant role in the body, secreting more than 50 hormones necessary for life. They are the first glands to fail when your life is on overdrive, or during prolonged or intense periods of stress. Unfortunately, my stress hormone, cortisol, was below normal levels.

So, I asked the normal question, "What kind of drugs will you give me for that?" It was silent, and then the doctor, who knew my relentless busy schedule, gave me "the look." I'm sure I raised my eyebrows, not knowing what she was thinking.

She said I needed to think seriously about making a lifestyle change. Diet, exercise, and supplements would help, but the root of the problem was stress, based on my overloaded schedule. In my mind I thought, "Yeah, right! That's not going to happen!" But after serious reflection, I owned up to the problem. This leads me to Step One of my three-step strategy to minimize, eliminate, or manage stress.

Step One: Change Your Lifestyle

This incident with the doctor was a wake-up call to take charge of my life and make some lifestyle changes. I had to really reflect and evaluate my schedule to come to grips with what was and wasn't important. What gave me the highest return? What was wasting my time? Who was wasting my time? Were there better and more efficient ways of doing things? What stress-busters did I need to intentionally incorporate into my life? After cutting back my schedule considerably, eating healthier, starting a morning swimming regimen, and taking supplements, I bounced back. Let me clue you in, not everyone will be happy with your lifestyle changes. But if you want to feel good and be healthy, you must make lifestyle changes.

It's interesting to find out what people do to reduce stress. These stress-busters range from reading, exercising, drinking a white chocolate latte, changing the kitty litter box, or getting a massage, to just sitting and doing nothing. We all deal with stress in many ways. At the end of this chapter, I will give you 101 stress-busters to help you manage stress, but remember, you must be intentional and incorporate them into your life on a regular basis. They can't be like the expensive exercise equipment you purchased, used diligently for two weeks, and then allowed to collect dust or used to hang clothes on.

Lifestyle changes can be just as simple as learning how to recharge, reset, and restore your brain. When my phone is close to 5% battery power or is completely dead, I'm looking for an outlet to plug my phone in, so it can recharge. When the battery is 100% recharged, I know I'm good to go for a good length of time. The opposite goes for our brain. When we're mentally fatigued, exhausted, brain fogged, or on overload, it's time to unplug it. You unplug by getting away from the computer screen, taking a walk, doing something different, getting a drink of water, laughing, moving from your workspace, or just stopping whatever you're doing. Even if it's for five minutes, your brain will be recharged when you go back to what you were doing. If I'm at my computer, i.e., working on this book all day, I try to stop every hour to go get up and get away. It's amazing how that little lifestyle tweak goes a long way.

When I used to have a cubicle job, I remember I took a lot of pride in my work ethic. I had the philosophy that if I skipped breaks or lunches, I would get more accomplished. Plus, I let everyone know that I was the office martyr who didn't take any breaks or lunch. However, I have discovered that quite the contrary is true; with breaks, you get more done. Remember to unplug and you'll be more refreshed and productive.

You must make lifestyle changes.

The second step to minimize, eliminate, or manage stress is to let it go:

Step Two: Let It Go

Now I'm not talking about the popular song from the Disney movie, I'm talking about letting go of things that you don't need in your life.

When I worked on Royal Caribbean cruise lines as an entertainer, I always enjoyed going to Jamaica (who wouldn't enjoy it?). In Jamaica, you quickly adopt their three-word philosophy, "No problem, mon." They have worry-free, care-free attitudes toward life and problems. When you're late for the bus, the driver says, "No problem, mon." When the bus breaks down, we all say, "No problem, mon." Of course, this attitude can create its own set of problems. However, we are discussing ways to eliminate excessive stress from our lives, and the "no problem" attitude –learning to "let it go"—is key.

The catty remark a co-worker said to you is not really that big of a deal unless you turn it into a big deal. Let it go! We need to take more time to pause and reflect over situations versus stressing out over them. I highly recommend going to You Tube or Vimeo and looking up Bob Newhart's video clip called "Stop It." You will laugh when you see how ridiculous it is when people allow stupid things in life to stress them out. Or you can buy the book, *Don't Sweat the Small Stuff*, by Richard Carlson. "Running on fumes, our minds become magnets for negative thinking. We might carry around unnecessary thoughts that get blown out of proportion," states "The Attitude Guy," Sam Glenn.

I used to really stress over people that got on my nerves. When I talked to my husband about it, he'd say, "It's important to LET GO of people who won't change." This doesn't mean to stop loving people or praying for them. It means DON'T TRY TO CHANGE THEM! We've known people all our lives that do the same things over and over and over. You give them advice, talk yourself blue in the face, and they don't change. My husband went on: "If you can change things for the better, then you should. If you can't change things for the better, then let it go. Don't obsess about it. Most of the time, people aren't going to change." This last sentence may seem a bit pessimistic, but it is true: Most of the time, people will do what *they* want to do, not what *you* want them to do—even if what you want them to do is the obviously right choice!

I've mentioned secondhand smoke and secondhand negativity, and now I'll mention secondhand stress. Don't inhale involuntarily other people's stress issues. It will increase your own stress level.

Many times, we even need to let go of "good" things. If you try to do it all and please everyone, the stress will catch up with you. I'm sorry to tell you that you're not Wonder Woman or Superman. Learn to say no and let go of some things. Yes, you might make some people mad, but if your stress level is high, you must take action steps to get great results for your health and attitude.

Step Three: Laugh More

The third step in the strategy is to laugh more. Laughter is a vital step in reducing stress. I already talked about this more extensively in Chapter 8: Laughing will reboot your brain.

In the book, *Heal Your Heart*, cardiologist Dr. Michael Miller did a fascinating study on the effects of stress and the heart:

> My colleagues and I designed a study to find out the potential link between positive emotions and laughter and the ensuing beneficial effects on the vasculature. We asked 20 healthy men and women to watch clips of two movies on different days. One, the violent opening battle scene in *Saving Private Ryan*, would be sure to evoke a stress response; the other clip was a funny scene from *Kingpin*, *There's Something about Mary*, or *Shallow Hal*. Because intense laughter is about 30 times more likely to occur in the presence of others, rather than when we're alone, we invited each volunteer to bring along a few friends when viewing the comedies. We tested the volunteers' vasodilatation before and after viewing each of the movie clips by constricting and releasing the brachial artery (located in the upper arm) with a blood pressure cuff and then measuring the blood vessels' function with an ultrasound.

The results Dr. Miller found were "remarkable," as he puts it:

> We found remarkable differences in blood vessel functioning depending on which movie the participants watched. Fourteen of the 20 subjects who watched the stressful drama experienced significant blood flow reduction due to vasoconstriction within 1 to 2 minutes of viewing the clip. On the other hand, 19 of the 20 subjects experienced vasodilatation and increased blood flow after laughing at the funny movie clip and again it happened quickly, within 1 to 2 minutes.... We were able to conclude that stress has a direct and immediate constricting effect on the blood vessels, while laughter has a direct and immediate dilating effect on the blood vessels. The results couldn't have been more impressive.

Begin consciously and deliberately to incorporate more laughter into your life if you want to change your attitude and reduce stress. By the way, I don't think I've ever seen a zombie on *The Walking Dead* ever laugh.

Stress on Your Job

Stress on the job is a distraction. It robs you of energy and it's exhausting. It affects teamwork, lowers productivity, creates a hostile environment, impairs your work performance, and stirs up negativity. According to an article in *Workplace Psychology,* "The cost of stress is $300 billion a year, due to absenteeism, turnover, diminished productivity, and medical, and legal, and insurance costs." There are countless reasons for stress on the job, and books written for all these different types of reasons. Therefore, I'm going to give you a simple three alternatives for dealing with stress on your job:

1. If you have a very stressful job and perhaps your job even fits into Forbes "Top 10 Most Stressful Jobs in the USA," then it's a must that you incorporate stress-busters into your life.

2. It's important on stressful days to remember your "WHY." Why did you become a teacher, doctor, or nurse? I was training a group from the Department of Agriculture and reminded them what they do is very important. The people they work with feed the world. You have to think how your occupation ultimately helps and adds value to other people. If anything, your paycheck puts food on your table. That's a great reason to work!

3. If you're so stressed by your job that your blood pressure is sky-high even thinking about going to work, or you are sick to your stomach at work due to the stress, then GET ANOTHER JOB! Start a job search, change your life, and start something new. Remember, Colonel Sanders started his multi-million business at the age of 62.

Let's review my 3-Step Strategy to minimize, eliminate, and manage stress in your life:

1. Make LIFESTYLE changes

2. LET IT GO

3. LAUGH more

Now let's look at 101 stress-busters to boost our attitudes.

101 Stress-Busters to Boost Your Attitude

"Brain cells create ideas. Stress kills brain cells. Stress
is not a good idea."

—Frederick Saunders

A few years ago, I met Heidi Hanna, New York *Times* bestselling author, at the "Association for Applied and Therapeutic Humor" conference. In her book *Stressaholic*, she writes about action steps and benefits to reducing stress (thanks to the author for allowing this use):

Rest to balance brain chemistry with strategic relaxation and recovery.

Repair to calm and nourish cells with energy-enhancing nutrients.

Rebuild to strengthen mental and physical fitness to optimize energy.

Rethink to optimize your perspective to see stress a challenge instead of a threat.

Redesign daily patterns to minimize overstimulation from the environment.

I know by now I must sound like a broken record, but you must **be intentional** and **take action steps** to change your attitude. Likewise, you must **take action steps** to minimize, eliminate, or manage stress in your life.

Here are 101 of my favorite stress-busters for you. Incorporating any of these stress-busters on a consistent basis will boost your attitude. (You can also check out my YouTube Channel for more stress-busters.)

101 Stress-Busters

1. Ask for help
2. Ask yourself, "Will this matter in a year?"
3. Bake chocolate chip cookies
4. Be prepared
5. Breathe deeply
6. Build a relationship with people who energize you
7. Burn a candle
8. Buy someone's groceries at the checkout lane
9. Celebrate something
10. Cheer your favorite sports team
11. "Chill Out"
12. Clean out a drawer or closet
13. Count your blessings
14. Concentrate on one thing at a time
15. Consciously tense and then relax every muscle in your body at bedtime
16. Cry on a friend's shoulder
17. Dance
18. Debrief
19. Do not obsess over things you can't control
20. Do not over-commit
21. Do one thing at a time

22. Don't rely on memory; write everything down

23. Don't speed

24. Don't sweat the small stuff

25. Do nothing at all

26. Drink stress-reducing teas: Passion Flower, Hawthorn, Siberian Ginseng, Chamomile

27. Eat 70% dark chocolate

28. Eat a protein-filled breakfast

29. Eat chocolate chip cookie dough (occasionally)

30. Exercise

31. Forget perfectionism

32. Forgive someone

33. Get a manicure with a friend

34. Get a pedicure with a friend

35. Get duplicate car, house, and work keys (You'll be glad you did!)

36. Get a massage

37. Get organized

38. Get reflexology

39. Get rid of annoying noises

40. Get rid of clutter

41. Get up 15 minutes earlier

42. Go for a walk

43. Go shopping (don't overspend)

44. Go swimming

45. Go to church

46. Go for a green smoothie, which will give you an energy boost

47. Go for ginger or wheatgrass shots to build immunity, which combats stress

48. Have a good cry

49. Have a heart-to-heart talk with someone

50. Help someone in need

51. Hide in a bathroom stall and just shut your eyes

52. Hike

53. Indulge in a favorite treat periodically

54. Invite Ben & Jerry over occasionally

55. Laugh with friends

56. Laugh out loud—very loud

57. Leave work at the door

58. Listen to a sermon

59. Listen to motivational podcasts

60. Listen to music

61. Listen to ocean waves or rain on your MP3 when you go to bed

62. Look at old photos or family movies

63. Make a budget and stick to it

64. Make a lifestyle change

65. Make a TO DO list

66. Make someone a home-cooked meal

67. Make someone smile or laugh

68. Make your own funny videos

69. Massage your temples

70. Mentally clock-out

71. Pause and Reflect

72. Plan a vacation

73. Plan your meals

74. Play a game with friends or family

75. Pray

76. Prioritize tasks

77. Put on uplifting music

78. Put something back you really don't need to buy

79. Remember that each day is a gift from God

80. Regroup

81. Remove distractions

82. Repeat positive affirmations

83. Ride a bike

84. Roll your shoulders in a circular motion

85. Say NO to extra projects

86. Simplify the holidays

87. Sing

88. Spend less

89. Stay hydrated with H20

90. Stretch

91. Take a day off

92. Take three deep breaths

93. Take a break from your computer screen

94. Take a brisk 10-minute walk

95. Take a hot bath with Epsom salts and light a candle

96. Walk on a beach or in a wooded area

97. Watch a comedian on YouTube

98. Watch a funny TV show or movie

99. Watch an old TV show from your childhood on YouTube

100. Write in a journal

101. ZZZZZZ's – Get More!

CHAPTER 10

GET HEALTHY

Does your attitude affect your health?

"A positive attitude literally makes your brain better."

—Jessica Stillman, Stanford Research Institute

Yes! Your attitude affects your health! According to the American Heart Association, a positive outlook means living longer and stronger. The study, which looked at 607 patients in a hospital in Denmark, found that patients whose moods were overall more positive were 58% more likely to live at least another five years.

According to a series of studies from the U.S. and Europe, "Optimism helps people cope with disease and recover from surgery. Even more impressive is the impact of a positive outlook on overall health and longevity. Research tells us that an optimistic outlook early in life can predict better health and a lower rate of death during follow-up periods of 15 to 40 years."

Cardiologist Dr. Cynthia Thaik states, "Prolonged bouts of anger can take the toll on the body in the form of high blood pressure, stress, anxiety, headaches and poor circulation. Research also shows that even one five-minute episode of anger is so stressful that it can impair your immune system for more than six hours. All of these health issues can lead to more serious problems such as heart attacks and stroke. Anger and hatred can be directed at yourself or at other people, but either way you lose when you allow these negative foods for the soul to take over."

This chapter is vitally important: **Your attitude affects your health and your health affects your attitude.** A year ago, when I had foot surgery, I was out of commission for four months, and it unfortunately brought the worst out of me. When you don't feel good, you're focused on yourself. I was frustrated not being able to function at my normal fast pace, I was worn out from hobbling on one foot, and I became very short-fused with people. Therefore, the zombie emerged many times with a sharp tongue, and of course I later felt bad because of it.

Let me refresh your minds as to how important it is to take care of your body. We want to be healthier, have more energy, and live longer. **I'll start with something very simple: Drink plenty of water.**

> **Your attitude affects your health and your health affects your attitude.**

A few weeks ago, I became very sick and the doctor ordered blood tests. The diagnosis was dehydration. It was a wakeup call to practice what I preach. Lack of water affects your health and can result in very dry skin, dizziness, rapid heartbeat, sunken eyes and cheeks, sleepiness, lack of energy, constipation, fainting, dark-colored urine, less frequent urination, and irritability. (Some of you reading this might be recognizing yourself right now!) Water dehydration also affects your mood. Remember, you should every day drink in ounces half of your body weight in pounds. For example, if you weigh 140 pounds, drink 70 ounces of water per day. Drinking water and brain function go together. It's important to fuel your brain. It's been said that 2% dehydration can make us stupid. According to *Psychology Today*, "Our brains depend on proper hydration to function optimally. Brain cells require a delicate balance between water and various elements to operate, and when you lose too much water, that balance is disrupted. Your brain cells lose efficiency." I have a post-it note on my desk which says, "Drink more H20." It prompts me to get up many times during office time to go and get a drink.

Some of you won't like this next recommendation, but here it comes… **EXERCISE.** Exercise will boost your mood.

Remember that Zombies like brains. Don't let them have yours! Your brain will keep you from exercising, because I know it is a mind game where exercise is concerned. I usually exercise in the morning; otherwise, everything else takes precedence over it and it never happens. Even if I say I'll do it in the afternoon, I don't. There are times I will wake up in the morning and say out loud, "I will feel better if I go swimming." I will repeat that several times between hitting the snooze button. (I tell myself this because I know from experience that I *will* feel better after swimming.) Finally, I drag myself out of bed (like a zombie), get to the YMCA, and as soon as I start, I'm good to go. I feel better, joints are moving, my attitude is spunky, and I'm ready to take on the world. Why is that? An hour earlier I didn't have that attitude. When your body moves, and you exercise, your brain immediately responds to change your attitude.

In fact, if you're at a computer, I want you to Google one of the most insightful Ted Talks I've ever watched: "The Brain-Changing Benefits of Exercise," by Dr. Wendy Suzuki, who is a neuroscientist. Dr. Suzuki talks about the change in brain chemistry as a result of exercise. She says three to four days of exercise each week will boost your brain and protect it from disease.

People get in a bad mood when they don't get enough Vitamin D, which is readily and simply available through sunlight. Take your sneakers to work and go for a walk in the sun when you have a break. Go outside, even for one minute or so, and get some rays. If you live in Iceland, start planning a Caribbean vacation.

You also have mood swings if you don't have enough fat in your brain. Better said, your brain functions better with good fat. Therefore, consuming omega-3 fatty acids is vitally important to keep you from becoming a zombie for the day. Besides taking supplements, here are some foods rich in essential fatty acids: Flaxseeds, walnuts, wheat germ, Alaskan wild salmon, sardines, chia seeds, Atlantic mackerel, trout, albacore tuna, anchovies, oysters, halibut, and avocados. It helps if you like seafood—notice all the cold-water fish in that list.

A good mood is the result of your brain releasing "feel good" chemicals. This occurs when neurotransmitters such as endorphins, dopamine, and serotonin are released. Neurotransmitters are chemical messengers that transmit signals from a nerve cell. You have the ability to change your own mood by doing things to stimulate the production of these chemicals. There are numerous neurotransmitters, but let's briefly look at the three different neurotransmitters that affect your mood:

Dopamine:

Dopamine is considered the "motivational molecule" and will provide, you got it, motivation. It enables us to plan ahead, focus on our goals, and be more productive. I call it the "high-five" chemical. Dopamine helps us feel enjoyment, bliss, and euphoria. It affects memory, mood, learning, sleep, and pleasure. You can raise your dopamine levels by eating foods high in tyrosine, the amino acid that dopamine is made from. Foods high in tyrosine include parmesan cheese, soy foods, lean beef and lamb, Brazil nuts, lean pork chops, bananas, almonds, avocados, fish and seafood, chicken and turkey, eggs and dairy, beans and lentils, and whole grains. Other ways to naturally stimulate the production of dopamine are to exercise regularly, get Vitamin D from the sun, get a massage, sleep more, listen to music, and take supplements for brain health.

Endorphins:

Endorphins are considered the "feel good hormone." They are natural peptide chemicals in your brain that help you feel more focused and pleasurable, less impacted by pain, and in a better mood overall. They are naturally released whenever you exercise, have sex, laugh, get Vitamin D from the sun, go shopping, get a massage, consume ginseng, get adjusted by a chiropractor, smell certain essential oils, and eat certain foods like dark chocolate, strawberries, sunflower seeds, bananas, Brazil nuts, cacao, chicken, grapes, spicy foods, and salmon, just to name a few.

Serotonin:

Serotonin is an important chemical and neurotransmitter in the human body and is known as the "happy chemical" because it contributes to wellbeing and happiness. It is also believed to help regulate mood and social behavior, appetite and digestion, sleep, memory, and sexual desire and function. Low serotonin levels have been linked to depression. Reducing sugar intake, getting more sun, massage, and exercise will stimulate serotonin levels. Foods to boost serotonin levels include the following: Bananas, basil, beans, blueberries, broccoli, brown rice, cacao, flax seeds, ginkgo, green tea, kiwi, maca, mandarins, parley, nuts, pineapple, Brazil nuts, salmon, spinach, sweet potatoes, cherries, tomatoes, and turkey.

As Hippocrates said, "Let food be thy medicine and medicine be thy food." Change your attitude today by taking control of your health with the food you eat. Since zombies like brains and I want you to protect your brain, I urge you to eat superfoods. Superfoods are good for your brain and have high anti-oxidant content which will fight free radicals in your brain and body.

Free radicals are nasty critters. They are actually molecules with an unpaired electron in search of another electron. They remind me of the Pac-Man game in the early video games, with little yellow creatures floating around trying to devour each other. These nasty free-radicals freely roam through your body seeking healthy cells, and can wreak havoc on your health. Let's reduce those free-radicals by eating superfoods like these: Dark chocolate, red beans, black beans, red kidney beans, pinto beans, cranberries, artichoke hearts, prunes (for those who like prunes), raspberries, strawberries, Gala, Red Delicious or Granny Smith apples, pecans, cherries, blueberries, cauliflower, broccoli, Brussel sprouts, almonds, avocados, cinnamon, salmon, wheatgrass, sweet potatoes, and flaxseeds. This is just a small list of superfoods; there are so many more. Just ask your friend, Mr. Google, and get a bigger list.

According to the Mayo Clinic, men need 30-38 grams of fiber a day and women need 21-25 grams of fiber a day. Remember the constipated zombie? Eating high-fiber foods will help keep the plumbing lines open. Here is a list of high-fiber foods (sorry, I don't like lima beans, which are high in fiber, so I left them out). The main point is to intentionally add more of these foods to your diet, because constipation equals crankiness.

Foods high in fiber include: Pecans, pistachios, walnuts, macadamia nuts, almonds, chia seeds, flax seeds, sesame seeds, dates, artichokes, raisins, red kidney and black beans, hummus, blackberries, raspberries, avocados, prunes, whole wheat pasta, canned pumpkin, pears, broccoli, quinoa, oatmeal, split peas, peas, okra, apples, spinach, kale, pomegranate, kiwi fruit, and oranges.

The last thing I encourage you to do for your health is to **get regular checkups**. I know women who never get mammograms, and some have paid the price by finding out late in the game that they're in stage four cancer. Sickness and disease will affect your attitude. If you don't have an appointment for a check-up, make one right now.

I hope this chapter has encouraged you to desire to work toward a healthier life. It's important to be intentional about doing things for yourself to feel better, look better, and change to a better mood.

CHAPTER 11

GET A STRONG FOUNDATION

Will faith help your attitude?

"But the things that come out of our mouth come
from the heart."

—Matthew 15:18

Jean Gatz is an awesome keynote speaker and award-winning author. I love something she says: "Your attitude is a visible indicator of your thoughts, your perceptions, your beliefs, your needs, and your wants. Your attitude is a visible indicator of how you feel about things and your attitude impacts how people relate to you, communicate with you, and whether they trust you or not."

Our attitudes form in our minds, flow from our souls, and spill out of our mouths. Find people with negativity spurting from their mouths and you know their inner selves are having struggles. Life can be difficult, people can be difficult, and the workplace can be difficult. In all the years I've worked, I've needed my faith in God to help me overcome attitude issues. When I've dealt with workplace zombies such as people who haven't treated me fairly or have been mean, I've had to "pray for those who despitefully use you." Dr. Earl Henslin, author of *This is Your Brain on Joy*, has done thousands of brain imaging scans on patients. According to Dr. Henslin, "Prayer for others, particularly prayer for their happiness and well-being, lights up the left prefrontal cortex—the happiness spot—of the human brain. In fact, few activities foster more feelings of joy than praying a blessing over someone else." Isn't that remarkable? Usually we would think, "Why pray for that guy over there? *I'm* the one who needs help!" But as we give to others, it is given back to us as well.

When I'm faced with people with negative attitudes, often I've needed to remember that "Love is patient, love is kind, it does not envy, it does not boast, it is not proud. It does not dishonor others, it is not self-seeking, it is not easily angered, it keeps no record of wrongs. Love does not delight in evil but rejoices with the truth. It always protects, always trusts, always hopes, always perseveres. Love never fails" (I Corinthians 13).

In Philippians 2:5, the Apostle Paul tells us, "Let this mind be in you, which was in Christ Jesus." Many versions say, "Let this attitude be in you. . ." Shouldn't we try to exemplify the attitude of someone who demonstrated love and sacrifice?

When I'm having a bad day, I try to remember to rejoice and be thankful for everything I've been blessed with. Lean on the One who created you and has a plan for you, even in the workplace.

Find people with negativity spurting from their mouths and you know their inner selves are having struggles.

CHAPTER 12

FROM A TO Z: ATTITUDE AND ZOMBIES

What is your attitude?

"My attitude toward others determines their attitude
toward me. If I smile at life, life smiles back at me.
I become a magnet of positive people, if I
radiate the same kind of energy."

—Anna Simpson

Taking small actions are the first steps into making adjustments in our attitudes. In conclusion, I hope that you live a life you can enjoy. The attitudes you have toward yourself, life, and others go hand in hand with enjoying your life. It is not easy to adjust to any workplace zombie attitude; therefore, you must be intentional about taking action to change those attitudes. Always remember, taking action in the right direction is the first step to bringing life to a dead attitude. If you're discouraged with the negative people you work with or with your job itself, then really take time to pause and reflect on whether you need to stay or leave. Sometimes the antidote for negativity is just remembering your "why." Your "why" may be to educate children, take care of patients, protect your community, and the list goes on and on. Maybe your "why" is right now to put food on your kitchen table and feed your family. Do you remember my moping zombie story? I'm so glad I never left the job at the hospital, as those frustrating years helped to mold me into what I would be doing down the road. It was a temporary training period for better things to come. I love what the late Maya Angelou said: "If you don't like something, change it. If you can't change it, change your attitude. Don't complain."

Your attitude is a priceless possession. According to Stanford Research Institute, "Our attitude is one of our most valuable assets. A positive attitude contributes to success in life more than anything else. 87.5 percent of people's success can be traced to their positive attitudes, while just 12.5 percent of their success comes from their aptitude, knowledge, or skills." Isn't that an amazing statistic?

> **Taking small actions are the first steps into making adjustments in our attitudes.**

You will draw more customers when you have positive energy and enthusiasm. Think about restaurants you frequent. If you get someone on the wait staff who drags himself up to your table and acts like the living dead, you will look at that restaurant's competitors the next time you go out to eat. Negativity in the workplace is a poor, unprofitable business practice.

Always remember that "CPR" can take you from the living dead to being full of life. C stands for choice. J Martin Khoe said, "The greatest power that a person possesses is the power to choose." P stands for perspective. Abraham Lincoln said, "We can complain because rose bushes have thorns, or rejoice because thorn bushes have roses." R stands for reboot your brain. Rick Warren said, "The way you think determines the way you feel. The way you feel determines the way you act."

Remember my story of being praised when I worked at Target? I worked twice as hard the next time I went to work because of my boss's ability to boost my attitude with his positive encouraging words. When you have high employee morale, productivity rises. People with great attitudes are magnetic—others are drawn to them. Here is a list of benefits of a positive attitude:

Achievement and success
Attracting good jobs
Attracting good things and good people
Better coping skills
Better problem solving
Better relationships
Boost in self-esteem
Better sleep
Career uplift
Confidence
Creating a pleasant workplace
Creativity
Dealing with problems professionally
Displacing fear in employees
Earning respect from others
Energizing self and others
Encouraging employees with problem-solving
Feeling good about yourself
Fighting depression
Giving momentum
Good relationships
Happiness
Health
Helping minimize, eliminate, and manage stress
Helping others
Helping to be more resilient during difficult times
High level of influence
Higher team morale and teamwork
Improving attitude of other employees

Improving customer relations
Improving decision-making
Improving interpersonal relations
Increased motivation
Increased bottom line
Innovation
Laughing more
Making the difference between giving up and going forward
Making your boss happy
More constructive thinking
More creativity
More friends
More resilient
More sales
Not as stressed as others
Overcoming challenges
People around you being happier
Producing energy
Productivity
Recognizing opportunities
Reducing stress
Respect
Strengthening relationships

"Your attitude determines so much about how you will live your life and how far you will go in life. I believe it even determines the overall quality of your life," said the late Keith Harrell in his book, *Attitude Is Everything.*

From now on, on television, in movies, on-line, in games, in life (or in your mirror), when you see zombies dragging themselves through life, reflect upon your own life:

* Are you grateful for every breath you breathe?

* Do others view you as a workplace zombie?

* Do you add value to other people?

* Do you spread the virus or do you infect others with your positive attitude?

* Do you regularly check your own attitude pulse?

* Do you know how to administer CPR to bring your dead attitude back to life?

* Are you taking care of your health so that your attitude is not affected?

* Are you gracious to the living dead?

* Do you need to laugh more in life?

* Do you need to renew your faith?

* Are you recognizing the good in other employees and showing appreciation?

* Do you act alive or dead?

As the character Red said in the acclaimed movie *The Shawshank Redemption*, "Get busy living, or get busy dying." It's our choice, isn't it?

On the one hand, we can drag ourselves through life like zombies.

On the other hand, we can live life to its fullest and be blessed with an awesome life. And that is what I want for you.

END NOTES

Chapter 1 – Negative Traits of the Living Dead

The Sixth Sense, Dir. M. Night Shyamalan. Hollywood Pictures, 1999. Film.

Chip Cutter. "People Are 'Ghosting' at Work, and It's Driving Companies Crazy," June 23, 2018. Retrieved from https://www.linkedin.com/pulse/people-ghosting-work-its-driving-companies-crazy-chip-cutter/, accessed January 19, 2019.

Chapter 2 – Zombies in the Workplace

Holly Black. *The Good Neighbors #1: Kin.* Graphix. 2008.

Google Dictionary, "Moping," 2019. https://www.google.

Catherine Clifford. "Unhappy Workers Cost the U.S. Up to $550 Billion a Year." *Entrepreneur* On-line Magazine. May 2015, Retrieved from https://www.entrepreneur.com/article/246036, accessed July 7, 2018.

John C. Maxwell. *Leadership Gold,* Thomas Nelson Publishers, 2008.

John C. Maxwell. *The 21 Irrefutable Laws of Leadership,* Thomas Nelson Publishers, 1998 and 2007.

Dr. David Rock, Dr. Al H. Ringleb. *Handbook of NeuroLeadership*. NeuroLeadership Institute, 2013.

David W. Ballard. "Change at Work Linked to Employee Stress, Distrust and Intent to Quit, New Survey Finds," *American Psychological Association*, May 24, 2017, Retrieved from https://www.apa.org/news/press/releases/2017/05/employee-stress.aspx, accessed October 22, 2017.

Lisa Quast. "Overcome the 5 Main Reasons People Resist Change." On-line *Forbes*, November 26, 2012, Retrieved from https://www.forbes.com/sites/lisaquast/2012/11/26/overcome-the-5-main-reasons-people-resist-change/#3f652833efdc, accessed December 18, 2017.

The Bible, Proverbs 22:24; 15:1

Allen Elkin. *Stress Management for Dummies*, IDG Books World Wide, Inc, 1999.

Donald Hicks. https://www.goodreads.com/quotes/66 39283-when-someone-would-mistreat-misinform-mi suse-misguide-mishandle-mislead-or.

Workplace Bullying Institute. "The WBI Definition of Workplace Bullying." 2018, Retrieved from http://www.workplacebullying.org/individuals/problem/definition/, accessed February 3, 2018.

Laura Stack. *Leave the Office Earlier*. Broadway Books. 2004.

Mark Fahey. "Facebook turns 12 – Trillions in Time Wasted." CNBC News Blog, February 4, 2016, Updated February 10, 2016. Retrieved from https://www.cnbc.com/2016/02/04/

facebook-turns-12--trillions-in-time-wasted.html,
November 28, 2018.

John C. Maxwell. *Sometimes You Win, Sometimes You Learn.*
Thomas Nelson Publishers, 2013.

Robert Bacal. *Perfect Phrases for Customer Service.* McGraw
Hill Education, 2011.

Robert Bacal. *If It Wasn't for the Customer, I'd Really Like
This Job.* Kindle Edition, 2011.

Chapter 3 – Adjust to Negative People

Victor Frankl. *Man's Search for Meaning*, Beacon Press, 1959.

Bible, Proverbs 25:21.

Chapter 4 – Enthusiasm is Contagious

Jungle Book. Dir W. Reitherman. Walt Disney
Productions, 1967.

H. Jackson Brown, Jr. *Life's Little Instruction Book.* Thomas
Nelson, 1991.

Frank Bettger, *How I Raised Myself from Failure to Success in
Selling*, Prentice Hall Press, 1947.

"Colorful Cape Air Makes Its Money Where the
Sun Shines." Kirby J. Harrison, April 17, 2008,
AIN Publications. https://www.ainonline.com/
aviation-news/aviation-international-news/2008-04-17/
colorful-cape-air-makes-its-money-where-sun-shines

https://en.wikipedia.org/wiki/Chewbacca_Mask_Lady

"Benefits of Fun in the Workplace," Mat Neasley, May 2015. https://thefundept.com/2015/05/benefits-fun-workplace/

Kevin and Jackie Freiberg. *Nuts: Southwest Airlines' Crazy Recipe for Business and Personal Success*, Bard Press, 1998.

Mike Veeck & Pete Williams. *Fun is Good: How to Create Joy and Passion in Your Workplace*, Holzbrinck Publishers, 2005.

Bob Ross quote cited in:
Stephanie Schnurr. *Leadership Discourse at Work: Interactions of Humour, Gender and Workplace*, Palgrave Macmillan, 2009.

Chapter 5 – Gratitude Will Change an Attitude

"Human-Focused Workplaces," GloboForce Press Release, GloboForce Research Institute. https://www.globoforce.com/press-releases/recognition-creates-human-focused-workplaces/.

Adreian Gostick and Chester Elston. *The Carrot Principle*, Free Press, 2010.

Chapter 6 – Power Words that Give Life

Dale Carnegie, *How to Win Friends and Influence People*, Simon & Schuster, Inc., 1936.

Chapter 7 – Help! A Zombie Bit Me!

Merriam-Webster Dictionary, "Perspective," https://www.merriam-webster.com/dictionary/perspective. 2019.

Oxford Dictionary, "Perspective," https://en.oxforddictionaries.com/definition/perspective. 2019.

John O'Leary. *On Fire*. First North Star Way, 2016.

Chapter 8 – Reboot the Brain

Charles Swindoll. *Grace Awakening*. W. Publishing Group, a division of Thomas Nelson, Inc. 2003.

Star Wars: Episode VI - The Return of the Jedi, Dir. Richard Marquand. Lucas Film Ltd., 1983. Film.

Pat Williams. *How to Be Like Walt*. Health Communications, Inc. 2004.

Groundhog Day. Dir. Harold Ramis. Columbia Pictures, 1993. Film.

C. W. Metcalf & Roma Felible. *Lighten Up*, Basic Books, 1992.

Dictionary.com, "Humor," https://www.dictionary.com/browse/humor. 2019.

Dr. Seuss. *One Fish, Two Fish, Red Fish, Blue Fish*, Random House, 1960.

Chapter 9 – Get Rid of Stress

Paul Huljich. *Stress Pandemic*, Mwella Publishing, 2012.

Oxford Dictionary, "Stress," https://en.oxforddictionaries.com/definition/stress.

Daniel Amen. *Change Your Brain, Change Your Body*, Crown Publishing Group, 2010.

"Stop It" Skit by Bob Newhart, https://vimeo.com/97370236.

Richard Carlson. *Don't Sweat the Small Stuff*, Hyperion, 1997.

Sam Glenn. *A Kick in the Attitude*, John Wiley & Sons, Inc. 2010.

Michael Miller. *Heal Your Heart*, Penguin Random House Publishing, 2014.

Steve Nguyen. "The True Financial Cost of Job Stress," *Workplace Psychology*, January 9, 2011. Retrieved from https://workplacepsychology.net/2011/01/09/the-true-financial-cost-of-job-stress/ (accessed November 17, 2018.)

Fredrick Saunders quote, https://www.azquotes.com/quote/550695.

Heidi Hanna. *Stressaholic*, John Wiley & Sons, Inc., 2014.

Chapter 10 – Get Healthy

Jessica Stillman, "A Positive Attitude Literally Makes Your Brain Work Better," Stanford Research Institute, On-line Inc February 15, 2018. Retrieved from https://www.inc.com/jessica-stillman/ stanford-research-attitude-matters-as-much-as-iq-in-kids-success.html (accessed November 17, 2018.)

"Circulation: Cardiovascular Quality and Outcomes," *Journal of the American Heart Association*, September 10, 2013.

"Optimism and Your Health," Harvard Health Publishing, Harvard Medical School, May 2008. Retrieved from https://www.health.harvard.edu/heart-health/ optimism-and-your-health. Accessed November 17, 2018.

"Toxic Emotions," *HuffPost* Dr. Cynthia Thaik, April 6, 2014.

Joshua Gowin, "Why Your Brian Needs Water," *Psychology Today*, October 15, 2010. Retrieved from https://www. psychologytoday.com/us/blog/you-illuminated/201010/ why-your-brain-needs-water, accessed November 17, 2018.

Wendy Suzuki. "The Brain-Changing Benefits of Exercise," *Ted Women* 2017, Retrieved from https://www. ted.com/talks/wendy_suzuki_the_brain_changing_ bene-fits_of_exercise?language=en, accessed November 17, 2018.

https://www.goodreads.com/quotes/62262-let-food-be-thy -medicine-and-medicine-be-thy-food.

https://www.mayoclinic.org/healthy-lifestyle/ nutrition-and-healthy-eating/in-depth/high-fiber-foods/ art-20050948.

Chapter 11 – Get a Strong Foundation

Jean Gatz. www.JeanGatz.com.

Earl Henslin. *This is Your Brain on Joy*, Thomas Nelson, 2008.

The Bible, Matthew 5:44; I Corinthians 13, Philippians 2:5.

Chapter 12 – From A to Z: Attitude and Zombies

Anna Simpson. *Create the Life You Dream About*. www. anna-simpson.com.

Stanford Research Institute Study, https://www.business-blogshub.com/2013/04/how-to-lead-with-attitude-part-1/.

The Shawshank Redemption. Dir. Frank Darabont. Castle Rock Entertainment, 1994. Film.

ABOUT THE AUTHOR

Desi Payne loves to inspire her audiences as a humorous motivational speaker and is known as the "Attitude Adjuster." She motivates leaders and their employees by helping them adjust their attitudes to create a positive work environment. Desi also likes to boost the morale of employees by helping them reduce stress in the workplace. Desi has over 25 years of experience as an entrepreneur, and is an international speaker and trainer with the John Maxwell Team. She is an award-winning entertainer and has worked with Royal Caribbean Cruise Lines and appeared with Ringling Brothers and Barnum and Bailey Circus. Desi and her husband, Craig, reside in Iowa; they have two grown children.

How good is your attitude?
Discover your AQ score today.
Visit DesiPayne.com/AttitudeQuotient

Would you like to reduce stress and adjust your attitude?
Subscribe to My YouTube Channel

Desi Payne

Does someone in your business or organization need an attitude adjustment?
If the answer is yes, Desi can help!

* Keynote Speeches
* Workshops
* Leadership Retreats
* DISC Personality Training
* High-Energy-Engagement-Education

Start the conversation at DesiPayne.com